Play Better Petanque

Andrew Gilbert

Published by Andrew Gilbert, 2024.

Table of Contents

Introduction

This book is definitely not for the big boys of Petanque! It is not designed to help the games of Dylan Rocher or Phillipe Suchaud or Quintais or Fazzino. Well, it might add to their arsenal of shots, but these are not the players this book is designed to help.

This book is for the average club player who wants to get better. Perhaps they even just want to know what they are doing wrong. I'd like to think it will take an average club player to the ranks of a decent regional player. After that, it always comes down to how much you want to put in the practice time.

How will it make the average player better? It will explain many of the myths in petanque and hopefully cure many of the bad habits we have all picked up over the years. And, trust me, we have certainly picked up a few bad habits over the years. Whether it be a persistent or (even worse) intermittent curve to one side when pointing or achieving a hit rate of around 20% when shooting. We all have bad habits that we have allowed to creep in over time.

Also in this book, we describe a

Revolutionary new way of aiming.

And

A Revolutionary new way of Pointing.

And

A Revolutionary new way of Shooting.

If that sounds like a far-fetched claim, then please reserve your judgement until you have reached the end of the book. I'm sure you won't be disappointed!

I suppose the Shooter has the worst part to play in this game. They know instantly whether the shot was a success or not. If they hit the target boule (especially with a carreau) and your team ends up holding the point, it was a success! If they missed the target boule or only 'winged it', it was not a success!

You might be asking "who am I to point out your faults?" I am an average player. Results would indicate we are above average in terms of the results we have achieved. My wife and I went on the New Zealand tournament circuit for a couple of years and we both made it comfortably into the top twenty in our national rankings. We have also played a few games in Australia and New Caledonia and England and Spain. We have both represented New Zealand. So, while we do not claim to be the top players in our area, we have actually been there and played with the top players in Australasia. I am also an arbiter or umpire of the game, trained by Mike Pegg and have umpired to an international level under the auspices of Andre Deramond.

What qualifies me to be a critic of your play? I am an observer. When I want to achieve something, I usually set goals and do the training for the task. The study side helps me to pick up the physical aspects of a task and my former career as a trainer helps me to understand the mental side of the game and where people are likely to fall down.

Let's get down to business. You don't need to hear about me. You want to hear how I can help your game.

Chapter 1 - Analysing your throw.

Let's assume you are an average club player that wants to get better!

Petanque does seem a fairly simple and straight forward game. So why can it be so frustrating?

Generally, the terrain is the deciding factor which can make or break our day because there seem to be so many different types of terrain around the world. Let's be honest, the techniques described in this book will help you become a better player unless you are playing on the toughest 10% of terrains. These are the terrains where the stones chips are an inch or more in size and sharp edged. There is every chance on those terrains that your boule will hit a sharp edge and kick sideways. All you can do there is put some backspin on your boule and hope it kicks in. These techniques are designed to help you improve on the rest of the terrains you will come across.

There are also a variety of shots available to the player to overcome the varying types of terrain. Later in the book we will go into some of the variety of shots available to the elite player and the somewhat smaller range of shots available to the average player.

Before we get too far into the book, let me say upfront that there will probably be one or two points, I raise, that you don't necessarily agree with. Believe me when I say I'm quite comfortable with that! You will take away from this book whatever you feel is appropriate.

There are a few things we can control, as a player, and there are also a few things we cannot control.

The big thing we cannot control is the terrain. It is what it is!

In France, they often have what I would call an unforgiving terrain. The rocks or pebbles they use for the surface they use seem to be over an inch long and at least a half inch across and they are complete with sharply angled edges. They are a nightmare for even the very best of players and it becomes something of a lottery when you pick your landing point, hit the exact spot and the boule kicks away at a right angle.

On these, the worst of terrains, there seems to be only one shot available to overcome the unforgiving terrain and that shot is the 'High and long lob' (often called the "Plombee"). This particular shot requires the player to be able to loft the boule up to perhaps six meters high and to have it land within a meter of the Jack. The reason for the very high lob is so that the angle of the boule in its descent is quite steep and the resultant rollout is minimized by the lack of forward motion in the boule. If that sounds technical, it is, but very few terrains demand this type of player dexterity.

About all I can say for this type of terrain is that it is the same for both sets of players. As a piece of advice, I could only suggest that you do everything you can to put some backspin on the boule and hope the back spin kicks in. In a worst-case scenario, the boule will hit the landing point and kick off to one side at a forty five degree angle. The terrain is what it is!

For the rest of the world (and most of France) the terrains range from a little more forgiving to a bowler's paradise. These average terrains generally respond to a boule with some spin applied so you should be able to throw in a predictable line.

Earlier, I noted that there are some things you control with your throw.

The first thing is your landing point. In a later chapter I'll go into some detail about the landing point, so I'll leave that until the later chapter.

The other two things you can control are firstly the amount of 'Lob' you put on a throw and the second thing is the amount of 'Rollout' you achieve. Together with the 'Landing point', these three items are very interrelated in that the higher the lob, the less rollout you will get and the 'landing point' of your boule now becomes quite important.

Your landing point was always important, but you perhaps did not realise that earlier.

It's just a suggestion, but I'd always suggest getting to the terrain a little early and throwing a few boules down on the terrain to decide whether a half lob or a three-quarter lob, etc is going to be your preferred average throw for the day. As I have said previously, we have played in Australia and New Caledonia and Spain and in England and, generally, the terrains are not too tough or unforgiving for the average player. It will only take a half dozen boules to make you aware of the 'rollout you are likely to get on any particular terrain.

In the course of the book, I will get down to explain in more depth about the height of the 'lob' and the 'rollout'. For now, let's talk in more general terms before we get down to details.

What of the game of Petanque worldwide? In the USA, for 2012, (the latest figures available) the FPUSA reported around 1800 members and estimated the total number of petanque players in the United States at around 50,000. In 2009 the French Petanque Federation (FFPJP) had over 310,000 members. (It helps, of course, that the FFPJP receives government financial support.) Thailand reports around 40,000 members. Spain has the most members of any European country outside of France — 30,000. The Netherlands, Belgium, and Germany each report around 16,000 players. Algeria and Morocco combined reported around 25,000 players. Altogether, at the end of 2009 the FIPJP reported about 530,000 card-carrying members in 88 countries. In many of the European countries there are professional, or semi-professional leagues and it is not uncommon for a player registered in one country to also play in a league for another country. Prizemoney varies greatly from one country to another, but it is not impossible for a talented player to make a tidy living from his petanque earnings.

As a side note I read recently that the number of players, in Europe alone, were currently at over two million. I can well believe that, however, I have not seen any further evidence to support that claim.

Pétanque was invented in 1910, in the village of La Ciotat, then an important port and industrial town, on the Mediterranean coast of Provence not far from Marseille. Living in La Ciotat was a shopkeeper and amateur boules player named Jules le Noir. Le Noir was stricken so badly with "rheumatism" that he could no longer do the running throw needed to play Jeu Provencal. In fact, he could barely stand. One of his friends was a café owner named Ernest Pitiot. Together, the two men developed a modified a version of boules that le Noir could still play. In the new game, players no longer threw their boules with a running launch. Instead, they threw while standing in a small circle. The new game eventually became known as *Pétanque* — a name probably derived from the Provençal words *pés tanca* meaning "feet planted" (on the ground). The new game quickly became extremely popular, and eventually surpassed Jeu Provencal to become the most popular form of boules in France.

Just to let you know, the new techniques aren't mentioned in the first two chapters of this book. But there is still a wealth of material to get you to understand before we get to that point. And don't miss out on Chapter Four! It covers the most important point in Petanque.

At the end of each chapter, I'm going to add a question on the rules along with the relevant number you could look at regarding that rule.

Could you be an umpire?

The situation is this. The Jack is thrown over the side string to the next lane by your opponents who said it is fine as it is an untimed game. What do you do?

Chapter 2 - Pointing and putting a curve on a Boule.

Let's get back to how you can improve your game.

Let's talk about the very basic throw or pointing technique.

It seems such a simple thing. Toss your boule down and let it end up close to the Jack. Oh, and don't forget to add some back spin. And don't forget to work out your landing point. And are you going to toss a half lob or a three-quarter lob? And what about having a boule of the correct size for your hand?

Let's just spend a moment on the correct boule size. There is no end of methods to get the correct boule size and they all seem to work within a few millimeters. As a rough guide I can only say that if the boule is too large for your hand you will tend to either grip the boule too hard or you will end up using what I would call the 'Dragon's claw' grip where your fingers are splayed around the boule rather than you being comfortable with the preferred 'straight fingered' grip. Go on to a few of the boule supply sites to get a feel for their hand/Boule size measurements.

Apologies to the left-handed players but I am a righty so all the diagrams etc are of myself. Hold them up to a mirror (or just use your imagination) to make them correct for you lefties.

Imagine this scene: there are three or four boules right in front of the Jack which is a couple of feet beyond the 'wall of boules' in front of you. How neat would it be to be able to aim a boule to the left of the 'wall of boules' and have the boule spin in from the left and nestle gently against the Jack. Here's how to do it.

I find it useful to go to your terrain and throw a boule alongside the string lines to measure the boule's progress. The amount it deviates over the string line is a really clear indicator of your prowess.

To get the boule to spin to the right requires the boule leaving from the back of the hand (right handers). For me, I find it helps to give the boule a slight flick and opening the fingers slightly, from little finger to index finger. but that will come down to your own preferred technique. Throw a few boules to get some consistency in your action. Note how easy this type of point really is.

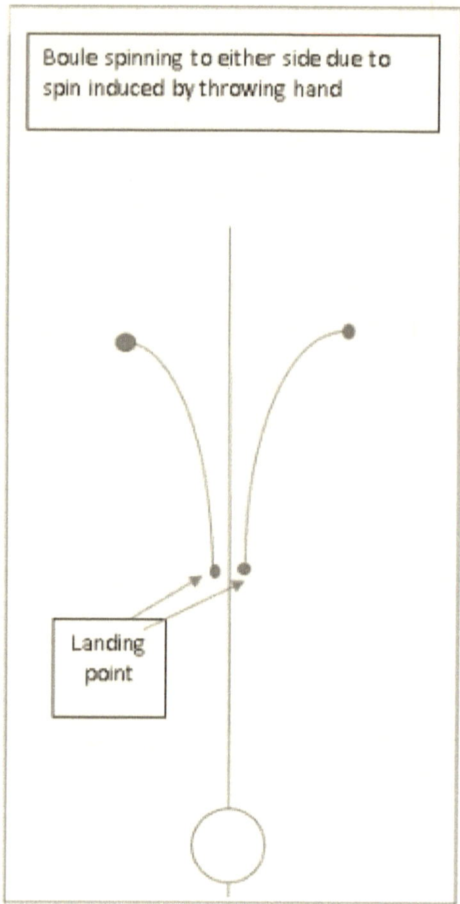

Dia 2.1 - The Boules in this diagram were pointed to the right-hand and left-hand side of the string and deviated perhaps a couple of feet to the right and to the left. If I had aimed a couple of feet to the left (Or to the right), they would have rolled out close to the Jack and on the string line. Which is the perfect counter for a wall of boules blocking your path to the Jack.

What will happen is the spin you impart is a counterclockwise spin (from above) and the spin will impact on the ground and make the boule move to the right or left in a progressively steeper curve.

Now how does the spin on a boule make a boule deviate? (This is important to be aware of). It's really quite a simple thing. When you toss a boule down the terrain it does not necessarily land on the terrain and then just roll out along the path it chooses. Let us imagine that the boule you threw travelled perhaps three meters in the air before landing. Be aware, the boule is still spinning with the spin you put on it. When it impacts with the terrain, the boule bounces up again as you would expect a ball to do. The boule is still spinning with its counterclockwise spin so the boule should kick just a little to the right due to the spin you put on it. When it lands again it will bounce again and deviate a little more to the right because the boule is still spinning in a counterclockwise direction. This will continue until the boule loses its forward momentum and comes to a stop. These small bounces are almost undiscernible until you actually closely examine the path of the boule, and you will see the small indentations (mini-Divots) the boule left along its ever-increasing curved path.

I hope you now realise why the boule wants to travel along the path you have applied the appropriate spin on. Another important thing to realise is that the effect on the boule when it stops spinning is that the boule is quite likely to now follow the undulations on the terrain. This means that the boule will likely only deviate, due to terrain undulations, in the last 5% to 10% of its travel. Before it gets to that point, the deviation will most likely be the deviation you put on the boule when you released it from your hand.

Now, how about a boule that will spin in from the right-hand side. Unbelievably the technique is very similar, but it is really just reversed. Allow the boule to leave from the inside of the hand (the thumb side) and open up the fingers from index to third finger. Note, this is the way I put a spin on the boule. Many purists would say that the correct way is to hold the boule as if you were throwing a straight boule but turn your palm inwards towards the side you want the boule to spin from. Whatever way works for you is fine as long as you are deliberately putting a spin on your boule.

What will happen is the spin you now impart is a clockwise spin (from above) and the spin will impact on the ground and make the boule move to the left in a progressively steeper curve. Again, throw a few shots to get a good feel of the control we are putting on the boule. It's a very handy shot to have in your arsenal of shots and it is well worth a little of your practice time.

Now spend a little time aiming the boule a couple of feet to the left (or right) of your target and practice making that shot work for you. Try it first by placing a spare boule at six meters and aiming your boule a couple of feet to the left for the boule's landing point. The rollout and the spin you placed on the boule should make the boule curl back to the right. When you can get comfortable with the results of that shot, move the target boule out to seven meters and practice again. Obviously, the boule will travel as far as the momentum you put on it, so you will have to adjust the amount of travel (or lob) you put on the boule. As a guideline, your boule will start to move with the spin you put on it as soon as it lands so you might want to think about a three-quarter distance landing point.

Now let's get to the heart of the matter.

<u>The boule will only travel in whichever way you send it</u>!

This is the real problem! If your boule is constantly (or intermittently) travelling to the right of your intended line, it is because <u>you</u> are putting a spin on the boule. The same is happening if your boule goes constantly (or intermittently) to the left. It is because <u>you</u> imparted a spin on it!

And if your boule sometimes goes to the left and sometimes goes to the right it is because <u>you</u> are putting a spin on it to make it go either way.

Usually, a bad habit or two has crept in over the years and it can be as simple as a cocked wrist sending your boule a different way than expected. As an observer I can say with confidence that the most common fault of imparting a side spin is by using what I call the "Dragon's claw" type of grip. This is the grip where the fingers of the hand are splayed apart. Usually this is to accommodate the wrong sized boule for your hand, but I digress. It's important the fingers are released as one unit to impart the smooth backspin on a boule. With the 'splayed finger' grip it becomes hard to get the fingers to work as one if they are all splayed. Sometimes you can get away with a straight point, in other occasions, you may release the little finger, or thumb, first which sends the boule into a right to left spin and the boule drifts to the right of the intended line.

Below are a few pics showing the best hand position for the release of the boule and after that there are a few pics of showing why the boule will travel to the left or to the right.

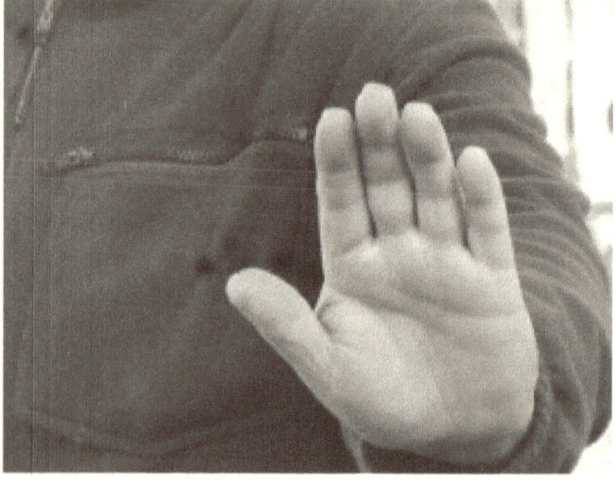

Diagram 2.2 The above two images show the moment of release of the boule. The straight (flat) hand is my preferred method as it tends to focus the mind on making sure the hand is flat at release. The pic on the right hand of the two shows the palm up method of release. I personally prefer the flat hand technique as sometimes the open palm method can seem like you are pushing the boule with the heel of the hand and with a slower delivery that is the net effect with the resultant loss of back spin.

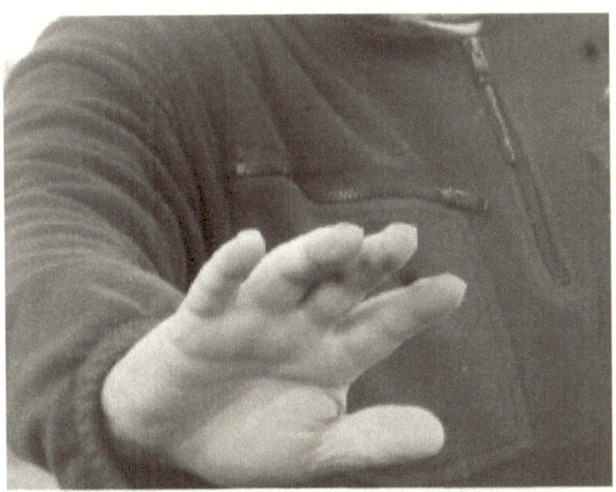

Diagram 2.3. The above release will almost always give the boule a spin to the right. It's almost the correct release for a boule to spin from left to right. Note, the hand is cocked inwards to the body.

With this hand position at release it's sometimes hard to say which way the boule will want to travel. The hand is cocked inwards towards the body. The fingers are splayed apart. The chances are that this type of release will send the boule anywhere but straight!

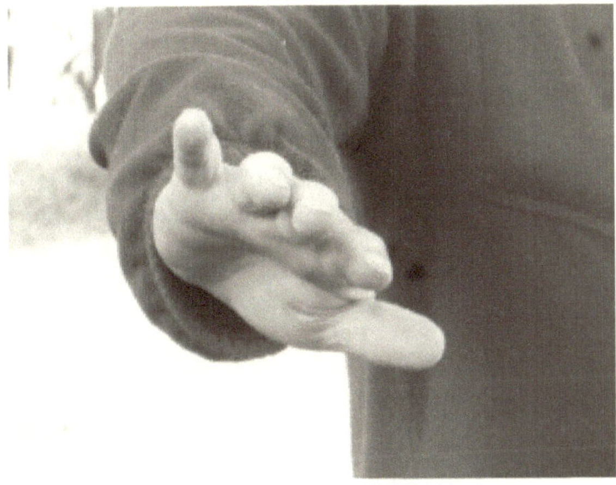

Diagram 2.4. With this hand position, again, the boule will want to spin to the side. It's almost the perfect position for a left to right spinning shot.

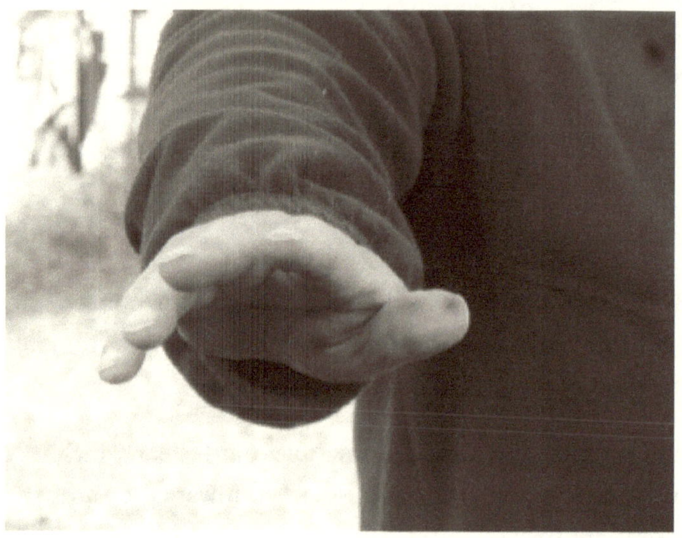

Diagram 2.5. With this type of release the boule will probably want to spin from right to left.

Later in the book I offer several practice routines to get you into using habits that will improve your game. I also suggest that you practice with a partner who can stand at the other end of the terrain. The idea of this is so that your partner can look at you as you play and mimic the hand position where you released the boule. If you can organise this type of practice partner, you should soon be made aware of where you could improve.

It's relatively easy to fix (and we will fix it) but it is important that you realise the boule will only go the way you send it.

Yes, I am aware that a deep-seated stone in the divot can send it awry but that usually only happens if you are unlucky, or you are playing on a very unforgiving terrain.

Let's get back to the spinning shot where you deliberately applied left-or right-hand spin.

From a personal point of view, I found that my spinning shot from left to right worked better for me than the other way. So, I practiced just that shot and it got me out of trouble on quite a few occasions. It got to the stage where I had to make a conscious decision, before I played the boule, as to whether I wanted the boule to go straight or come in from left to right. And of course, as I got further into a weekend of tournament play occasionally, I put totally the wrong spin on a boule and the boule started two feet to the left and ended a further two feet to the left as I had put the spin for a straight shot on a boule I had aimed to the left. It happens!

All players should now realise that the spin we impart on the boule has an instant effect on the forward motion of the boule when it hits the landing point.

Now let's look at the shot we try to play most often. The straight-pointing shot!

If we spin the ball from the back of the hand and it goes to the right, then we spin the boule from the inside of the hand, and it goes to the left we should spin the boule from our fingertips and keep the fingers straight and the ball will go straight. Yes, I'm sure you know this, but it is still the main reason why players do not improve!

Let us go back a couple of steps and have a think about this. If we are always getting a curve on our boule, it is because *we are putting a curve on our boule*. Let us look at that one more time.

If we are always getting a curved rollout on our pointing boule,

it is because we are actually putting a curve on our boule.

It's really not that hard to pick up on where we are going next.....

Ignore that thought for a second and let's go and try tossing a boule that stays straight!

Hint 1. Keep the fingers straight.

Hint 2. keep the fingers together.

Again, Using the string line on the terrain try and throw a straight-line point.

There is another point I'd prefer to leave to the relevant chapter in the book, but I will mention it here as a foretaste.

Shift your Bum, Chum!

Being ultra-polite I could rephrase that as 'Get your hips out of the way'. Later in the book I will get to a chapter on aiming your boules in a new way. For now, an important part of overcoming a bad habit is that we forget to shift our hips a couple of inches to the left so we can swing in a nice smooth and straight-line arc instead of swinging our arm in a curve around our hips and then expect any consistency in our aim.

Be aware that the slightest variation in our release point (in a 'round the body' type of swing) can result in a quite different result (See Diagram below). This is the leading cause of players being unsatisfied with the shoot or point. Let me take that a little further. As you're playing time goes on, and your arm gets a little more tired, you should not be surprised that your results become more and more erratic. Look at the diagram below and think about how you feel towards the end of a long day's play. Are you really surprised at the results? Remember, with the speed we bring our arm forward to the release point, there is only perhaps a milli-second between the three release points!

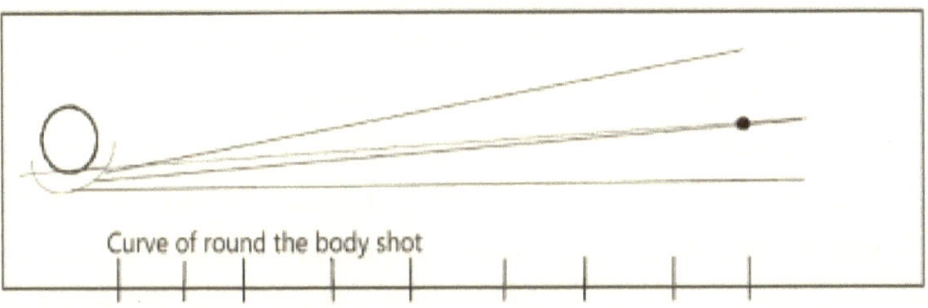

Diagram 2.6. With a 'round- the body type of arms swing, you are very reliant on achieving the same release point. The above diagram shows the wildly different results you can achieve if you miss getting the identical release point in your forward swing.

Imagine, if you will, a darts player, or a Snooker player, or an Archer.

One thing they all have in common is a straight line of arm or consistent pivot point with a straight line of arm. If they had to swing their arm around their body, first backwards, then in a forward motion duplicating the arm action of the previous backward arm swing, they would have a difficulty. Yet we club players are expecting to achieve consistent results with an inconsistent swing action.

So, let's have a go at pointing a straight boule.

Remember!

Hint 1. Keep the fingers straight.

Hint 2. keep the fingers together.

Hint 3. Get your hips out of the way!

The straight point is the shot we should be playing most often, so let's spend a few lines getting it correct.

Hold your hand palm up and fingers extended and together. Place the boule in your hand and curve the fingers up to grip the ball. How tight to grip it? If you turn your hand so it becomes palm down facing, the boule is being held sufficiently tightly if it doesn't drop from your hand to the ground. Don't be tempted to put a death-grip on the boule. When you release the boule, you want it only to roll against the tips of the fingertips to impart some level of back spin. If you hold the boule too tightly you will likely end up tossing the boule in a nearly vertical motion and that can be a headache of its own making!

The next item to think about is the amount of distance you initially toss the boule before the boule hits the ground and continues on. It doesn't really matter as long as you put the correct backspin on the boule. Let me expand on that a little. As this book is designed for the average petanque player, you will already have some Idea of which distance you prefer to lob the boule and how much you then let it roll.

Diagram2.7. Note: Fingers straight and held together!

Remember, from the passage that explained why a boule will move to the right, we discussed that the boule is actually executing a series of little skips. In this example of a straight-line boule, when the boule makes contact with the ground, the backspin you have applied will make the boule want to go forward in a straight line.

On a personal level I have played on most types of surfaces. When I am stood in the circle I usually decide approximately where I want the boule to land and how much I want it to roll thereafter. What I don't do is then work out the relative distances divided by the height of the half lob, allow a little for the curve of the earth, whichever way the wind is blowing and then allow a little extra depending on which political party is currently in power. I simply look at the shot or point I want to make! I then allow my brain a second to process the shot and then fire the shot on its way. Your brain is very good at making these kinds of decisions. If you have already made one pointing decision, then you have probably already made a thousand pointing decisions in your petanque life. Don't get in the way of your brain. It's usually pretty good at these kinds of things!

The only thing that should make any difference is the type of terrain you are playing on. The type of terrain will determine how much 'rollout' you wish to achieve.

Put a Jack around six meters away, perhaps a couple of inches away from the string line. And stand with your throwing arm a similar distance from the string. Throw the boule and see where it ends up. A pointing shot. This is really the most fundamental thing a petanque player can do. Shouldn't we be making an effort to get this right?

How did it go? If the boule went to the left or to the right of the string it should only mean that you are putting a curve on your boule when you release it!

As an aside, when you are playing on this more average type of terrain keep an eye out for this result.

IF you pick your landing point and hit it fairly well, you can expect the boule to travel forward in a straight line. If it does not continue in a straight line, then one of two things has happened. Firstly, if your boule deviates in a <u>straight line</u> to either side, then the chances are likely that you hit a sharp stone in the depths of the divot you made which then made the boule divert or deflect into its new direction. If your boule hits the divot and then proceeds to <u>curve left or right</u>, the chances are that you put a spin on the boule when you released the boule.

Later in the book I will go into more detail about the various types of shot available but at this point, let's get into the techniques of a simple 'pointing' game.

Let me offer another way of realising why we don't point to a target that well. Imagine you are driving a car and you have a vehicle some fifty yards ahead of you. What is happening is that both of your eyes are making the judgement of the vehicle being fifty yards away. It is a thing called *Parallax*. (Sometimes called Parallax deduction or Parallax distortion). Both of your eyes are getting an image of the distant object and your brain is doing the calculation that the object is fifty yards away. This is how we judge distance as humans. If you don't believe me, try putting an eye patch on one eye and then try and walk around the house. If you are a normal person, you won't get very far before you end up bumping into the corner of a wall etc. If you like, it is exactly like getting two images from separate points and your brain does the calculation automatically. When you are aiming to find the (target) line of something, what you do not need is both eyes to send an image to the brain. You only really need one eye to do the work. This is why the telescopic sights on a rifle only have one lens for the eye to focus on and not two lenses. You use your dominant eye to get the line. You may then use both eyes to work out the distance to the object, but you only use your dominant eye to get the actual target line. It is the same thing with working out your target line in petanque.

We were talking about getting a straight point. If you can get this simple technique, of a straight point, reasonably consistent, your overall game is likely to improve <u>dramatically</u>. Also, it will have an amazing effect on your level of confidence.

Again, using the string line on the terrain try to throw a straight-line point. Again, throw a few boules. Surprise, surprise, you can throw a straight point!

Remember the three things you have to do:

Hint 1. Keep the fingers straight.

Hint 2. keep the fingers together.

Hint 3. Get your hips out of the way!

If you can put five minutes practice into the point where you use the above hints, you should be throwing a straight boule!

Many players will be pleased enough at this time, knowing they can now throw a straight point.

I have coached a number of club players who have only now realised their throwing technique has been the accumulation of years and years of bad habits creeping in. Generally, few clubs have anybody willing to act as an observer who can make recommendations to amend your throw. If you think about it, the only thing we actually do, physically, in petanque is throw the boule. Isn't it appropriate that we start to get that better?

Before I move past this point (that's a pun, by the way) let me talk briefly about making an adjustment.

If you throw the first boule and it travels a meter past the Jack, you only have two options to decide between. You can either lob the boule higher and go for the same landing point or you bring your landing point of the travel closer to your circle. If the boule stops a meter short of the Jack, then you can opt to either pick a landing spot farther away for the circle or you can opt for the same landing spot and have a lower trajectory on the 'lob' part of the throw. The player I usually play with the most often is my wife. And if she points a boule that goes way too long or way too short, she will only hear me say 'make the adjustment' and she knows to amend her landing point. As a sidenote, all terrains will try and fool you. You make the perfect landing point as per how you worked it out in your head and the boule goes a couple of meters long. It happens! You possibly hit a larger stone and the boule bounced higher and longer. So, get on with the next throw and move on.

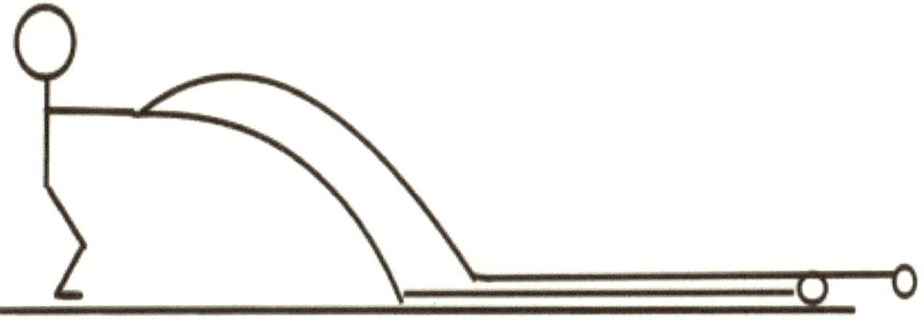

Diagram 2.8. shows the method of adjustment if the boule travels too far or too short of the jack.

There is one other thing to talk about before we move on further. When you hold the boule in your hand ready to deliver the point or shooting shot, we should remember how far we want the boule to travel. For longer distances it is quite common to 'flick the wrist' in your throw. As I have covered other facets of the throw, I'll take a punt at explaining this maneuver. As you lift your arm into your backswing you need to fold your wrist position in towards your under- forearm. See the diagram below.

Diagram 2.9. This shows the 'clenched wrist' position where the wrist is held back into the angle of the forearm to achieve a 'flick'

Keep this 'clenched wrist' position into the back swing and as you accelerate forward to the release point allow the boule to roll off your fingertips to get the desired backspin.

Diagram 2.10 showing the hand position at release, to achieve maximum backspin.

It initially may seem counter-intuitive, but most players would push their opposite arm behind them to give them some sort of balance mechanism,

As you move your right arm forward into the forward swing, keep your arm in the 'clenched wrist' position. When you are ready to release the boule, bring your hand forward to the position where it will roll off your fingertips (to get backspin). This action at the release point of your throw will give the boule some added impetus at its discharge and will result in the boule travelling further due to the increased impetus it now has. I've taken a note from another site here and would add the following:

Keep your throwing arm straight. Once the arm moves inwards (bends) the result is that you then put a spin on the boule to the left or right.

Diagram 2.11. If you bend your arm during your forward swing, you do tend to lose a lot of accuracy in the direction of throw.

Don't gradually uncurl your wrist/arm during the forward swing. Keep it 'cocked in towards your forearm' and then snap it forward during the last actual movement of your forward swing before releasing the boule. This is the way most players will get an extra impetus to their swing.

Could you be an umpire?

Team A captain picked up the jack believing that all boules had been played. However, Team B still had a boule left to play. The jack was not marked, so I know the player who threw it should receive a yellow card. But what about Team B who is still holding a boule?

Chapter 3: Aiming straight!

I do watch quite a bit of the French petanque on YouTube. When the players are really on form, it seems almost that one team points a boule in close and the other team then shoots it out. The first team then points again, and the second team shoot it out again. This repeats itself until the end is completed. If the shooting team is lucky enough to get a carreaux, then the roles are reversed. At the completion of the end, there are boules all over the terrain. There will usually be half of the boules over the dead boule line and perhaps only a couple or three boules within a meter of the Jack.

That is fine for the top players but we mere mortals almost seem to play a different game. With the top players there may only be two or three boules within a meter of the head when it comes to measuring. For us mere mortals there may be six or eight boules within three feet of the head because we play more of a pointing game with the occasional heroic club member that fancies him/herself as a shooter. In that case there may well be three or four boules that are on or beyond the dead ball line.

A reminder that this book is not for the top tier players! It's for the average club player who wants to get better! I do seem to be repeating that phrase often, but it is important to realise this guide is for the average player and not the top echelon of players.

Now I'd like to introduce you to a new way of Aiming. It is novel! It is accurate! And it will improve your pointing and shooting.

Currently we see ordinary club members standing in the circle with a boule in their outstretched hand working out where to aim for. Then they, in one quite unsmooth motion, swing their arm in a semicircular motion behind their back. The next facet of the swing is that they bring the arm and boule swooshing forward, again in a semicircular sweep. So far so good! They bring the ever-increasing arm speed back up to their release point and let the boule go.

Yeay!!

Unfortunately, the release point of the boule bears absolutely no relationship to the point they were so intently focused on when aiming or even the position they held their boule in when they were trying to aim the boule.

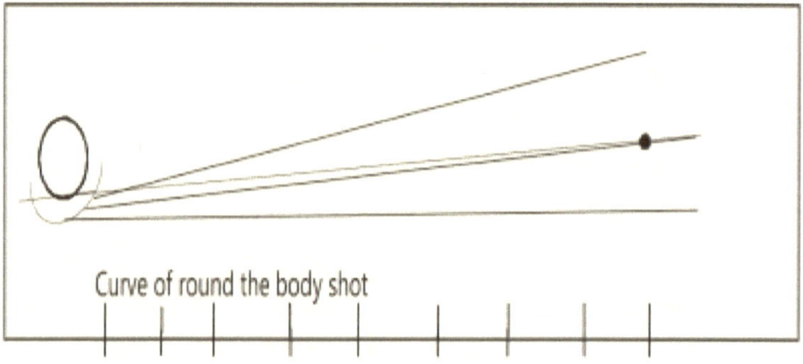

Dia 3.1 – Shows the release points of a 'round the body' shot. The gap between the three release points is down to a millisecond but the results are wildly different. Yes, we have used this diagram before, but it is important you realise the difference this 'round the body' shot can give.

Let me take that one point further. Most players will carefully walk up the terrain and carefully repair one divot, as per the rules. What they don't seem to realise is that they then go back and stand in the circle and 'aim' their boule. Surely it would be more beneficial to carry out this operation the other way round. Surely it would be more appropriate to first stand in the circle and pick out your landing spot (more on that point, later). Once you have decided where to land your boule, then go up the terrain and repair any divots that may affect your landing point. Yes, there may be players out there who say they were actually repairing a divot that may eventually be on their 'rollout path'. I still maintain that the bulk of club players will miss their 'repaired divot' point by a foot or more. I've spent countless hours as an umpire and by observing these players and their foibles, well, it helps to pass the time.....

When they release their boule, the eventual landing spot is often within a couple of feet of the divot they so carefully repaired a few moments ago. 'Within a couple of feet' is a euphemism for "what a waste of time repairing that divot was!" If you don't believe me, stand down the terrain when a player repairs a divot and then watch where their boule actually lands. A good practice routine is to repair a divot and then try and land where the divot was. You will be surprised how many times the average player will miss their 'repaired divot' by a couple of feet. An excellent practice routine is to try to land your boule in a divot hole. Because the divot is usually only a couple of inches wide, and four or five inches long, it becomes a real test of your accuracy at picking your landing point.

I'm talking again about the top tiers of players when I say they very seldom aim! Whether they are pointing or shooting they generally gaze intently at the aiming point (or landing point) for a second and then they release the boule to do its thing. They allow their brain to do all the calculations. They allow their brain to calculate the correct amount of lob. They allow their brain to sort things out. They are rarely seen holding the boule out in front of their dominant eye to get some 'read' on the terrain.

For us mere mortals, we probably don't play to that level often enough for our brains to get trained. That is not true, actually. Sorry to disappoint you, in actual fact, our brains will work with anything we have done more than a few times. It becomes a habit in your mind. And once something becomes a habit, it also becomes very hard to change that habit unless you make a conscious decision to change that habit. Getting hold of this book is a very good way to change some of your habits on the terrain by replacing them with new habits.

First, let's look at the average player, and by this I am probably talking about most players outside of the top tiers of players. I spent the weekend playing at the New Zealand Interclub champs and I was playing for one of the teams, so I was not able to look on as a disinterested umpire. As usual I took my preferred spot at the target end of the terrain and off to one side (as per the rules). I watched with interest at the beginning of the weekend when a player walked into the circle (after repairing a divot). On most occasions the player would hold out the boule at arm's length in preparation for their shoot or point. So far so good. For the most part they would not be that accurate as they were typical club players. The biggest thing I noticed was that they would then take their next shot, or point. And they would be holding their boule out at a quite *different* point, relative to their shoulder/eyeline! It's the first time I had been able to actually observe this behaviour. It's probably because I was in the middle of writing this book that I took the time to notice their strategy or style, or lack thereof! Our games were all timed, so I had an average of an hour to see this behaviour repeated and repeated. And it was pretty much the same in the next game, and the games after that. Eventually we ended up playing the top team in our last game on the Sunday. It was somehow comforting to see how they handled their time in the circle. None of the holding the boule at eye level to get a read on the terrain. Their shooters were pretty good as a regional level shooter (Hitting 2 out of 3) and they all seemed to have some idea of an overall strategy. We were beaten 13-10 but it was almost enjoyable to get beaten by a better team!

Back to the question! So why do we stand in the circle looking hopeful as we try and aim this boule to its intended target. Is it because it's what we have always done? Because it's sometimes worked before? Because we are, so far, content to be average club players! Because that is our habit pattern! Because it usually seems to work?

Okay, I said I had a revolutionary way of aiming the boule. Here it is

It's too late to aim, for us average people, once we stand in the circle. here is the new way of aiming. It's radical and it's deceptively simple.

Stand beyond the rear of the circle. Have your eyeline... No, let me take that back one step. If you are right-handed with your pointing, generally your right eye is your dominant eye. Have your right eye at the end of the line between the target (Jack etc) and the right-hand edge of the circle and your right eye. You can see a clear and straight line to the target.

For all of the left-handed throwers, your left eye is the dominant eye, and you need to be lining it up with the *left-hand* side of the circle.

Again, you are standing behind the circle. You have your <u>target</u> and the <u>right-hand edge of the circle</u> and your <u>right eye</u> all in a line. You now have the ideal line for your throwing arm.

And here is another point for you to think about. Your target line is not a foot wide! If you have your target line a foot wide, then there is every chance you will miss the target! Your target line is a centimeter wide or a half inch wide. If your eyesight is not that good, get the target line as small and defined as you can. The more accurate the target line is, the more accurate your pointing and shooting will be!!

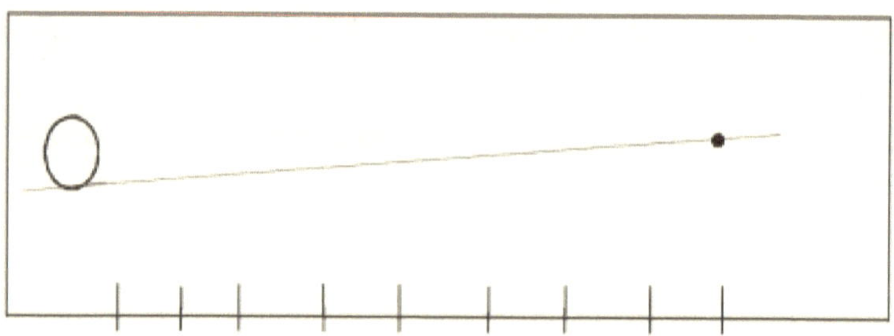

Fig 3.2 Shows a terrain diagram with the jack at approximately 8 meters. The line from the right-hand edge of the circle to the jack (and extended) is an imaginary line for the player to sight between the right-hand edge of the circle and the jack (or target boule). If you stand with one eye directly <u>behind</u> the right-hand edge of the circle and the target, it automatically gives you a sight line on which to pitch your boule and pick your landing point. When you step in the circle your hand will automatically line up provided your throwing hand is above the right-hand edge of the circle.

Pick out your landing spot. You may want to repair a divot **after** you have picked your landing spot, that's fine. If there is no divot to repair, that's even better. Choose your landing spot carefully. You are looking for a piece of the terrain that is firstly on your line between your eye and the circle and the target point. The second thing you are looking for is a piece of the terrain that is fairly smooth and even.

Pick out something nearby as a reference for yourself.

Perhaps there are a couple of divots on the terrain at just short of your landing point distance, and you think that a couple of inches beyond the two divots and a couple of inches to the right is your preferred landing spot. Then that becomes your targeted landing point. Anything that will give you a reference is fine.

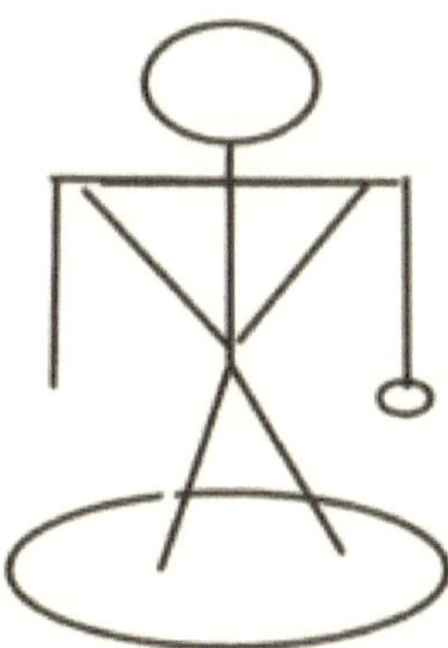

One advantage of picking out your landing spot is that your target may be nine meters away, but your landing spot may only be four or five meters away. It has automatically become a whole lot easier to hit a target (landing point) at five meters away rather than the target at nine meters away.

Now step back into the circle and this is the key for you to remember.

Your throwing arm, shoulder and hand should be directly above the right-hand edge of the circle.

Get used to this position. It may mean you have to stand two inches inside the circle. It may be three or four inches inside the circle. It will be slightly different for everyone. But that will become the only thing you have to be conscious of, position wise! As you practice this technique you will find that your feet will automatically stand in the correct position, inside the circle, by habit. You already have your targeted landing point in mind, so that is the only thing you have to focus on. If the Jack is out at nine meters and your selected landing point is at five meters, then you already have a much closer target (The landing point) to aim for. Think about that as just one of your advantages.

Diagram 3.3 shows the correct position for the 'new way of aiming' where the right (or throwing arm) is above the right-hand side of the circle. Obviously, it is reversed for the left-handed throwers.

As a suggestion, your leading foot should be aimed a couple of inches to the left of your target. Forget the old adage that your foot should be aimed at the target. That will only promote a round-the-body shot for the right handers. You already have your landing point in mind. Remember to push your hips out of the way so you have a straight arm swing. Swing the boule and see what happens.

Already we have talked about the three things you need to remember for a straight point.

Hint 1. Keep the fingers straight.

Hint 2. keep the fingers together.

Hint 3. Get your hips out of the way!

All of the above are generally things that have crept in over the years as bad habits and they have been so gradual they were unnoticed.

One side benefit of lining up your throw with the circle and your landing point is that you will already have a great idea of where you need to stand in the circle. This so much better than simply walking up to the circle and standing in it and then deciding which direction you could possibly throw the boule.

So, the key to practicing this technique is this:

Set up 2 boules at the six-meter mark around two feet apart, and one boule approximately midway between the two and perhaps a foot or so beyond.

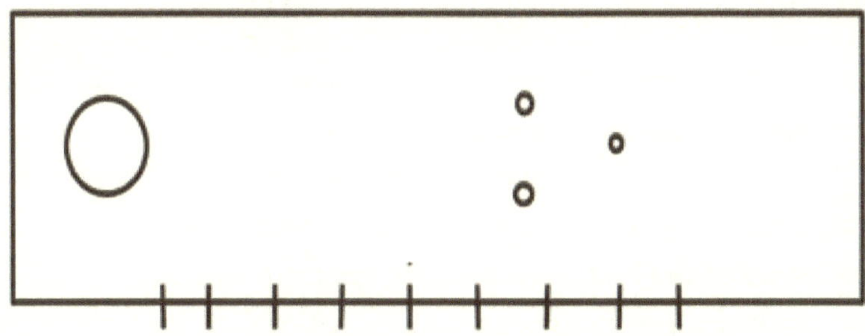

Dia 3.4. shows the practice routine for aiming straight.

Stand behind the circle to select your landing point, and then step in the circle and aim for the boule in the middle with a straight point. Remember, you are only going to point your boule to the target boule. Try it for three goes. If you are happy with the result, move the front row of boules to around 15 inches apart and try again. When you are happy with that, move the front row of boules to twelve inches apart and try again. When you get confident you should be able to have the front row of boules no more than six inches apart and still be confidently capable of hitting or resting on the target boule. Remember, what we are practicing here is the throwing of a straight boule to a predetermined target. The straightness of the shot and distance of the shot is mainly determined by the landing point you picked out and the manner in which you hold the boule in your throwing hand. I always find it helpful to work with a partner here who can tell you if you missed your landing point or if you inadvertently put a side spin on the boule. The partner has a whole different view on the proceedings if they stand at the far end of the terrain. They can indicate by a hand movement whether you accidentally put a side spin on the shot. Or if you did a round-the body-semicircle shot etc. Quite often it is an indicator of a poorly executed shot if your throwing hand is all splayed out at the completion of your throw. This, again, is something your partner at the other end of the terrain can help with.

I suppose the main difficulty with this new method of pointing is hitting your landing point every time. If that is a problem for you, try this. Mark your landing point only a couple of meters from the circle and try again. You may need to put a little more 'oomph' behind the throw to make the boule reach the target from such a short landing point. Again, believe it or not this is also a helpful device for when you prefer a 'Quarter lob shot'. When you are happy with your progress, then increase your landing point to perhaps 2.5 meters and try again. When you are confident at 2.5 meters, mark your landing point at 3 meters and so on. It's like any other new technique you try, it will take time and practice. But if you genuinely wish to improve your standard of play, this is definitely the way to start your advancement.

Also be aware that your landing point is not <u>absolutely critical</u> to the success of the throw. If you are an inch away from your planned landing point, then it only means you will be, at most, a couple of inches away from your target. That is often an improvement for a pointing throw!

Remember the key to your improvement is:

Throwing the boule in a <u>straight line</u> at a selected <u>landing point</u> and the resultant <u>rollout is also straight.</u>

Anything less than the above means you are not improving anything.

Now let's talk about the landing point.

If you are pointing to the Jack, the ideal line for your throw is directly in line with the Jack and perhaps around the halfway mark. Suppose you look at the landing point and your target line you notice there are a few noticeable stones in your way.

Firstly, I don't think it would be out of order to walk up the terrain and press down one of the stones as part of your 'repairing a divot' routine. That is what the top players do!

Alternatively, if you are using the point to get near the Jack, does it really matter if you are an inch or so to the left or right side of the Jack? A boule six inches short of the Jack is still going to be a visual or mental block for your opponent.

Could you be an umpire?

Team A throws an illegal jack.

Team B picks up the circle, takes it back approximately 1 meter and proceed to throw the jack from the circle. The jack lands in the middle of the piste and it is pointed out to the player of Team B, by one of its team, that he should 'place' the jack. The player then picks up the jack again and places it on the edge of the piste, right next to the string.

Is it legal for a team to place a jack twice?

Chapter 4 The most important point in petanque

....is your landing point!

It is so important we have devoted an entire chapter to it!

Your landing point will determine how far your boule 'rolls out' before coming to a total stop. It will also have quite some influence on the direction of travel if you don't remember to apply some backspin!

I can't emphasise that enough!

So many players concentrate on just the target boule, or target Jack, that they completely ignore the significance of their landing point. Your landing point is the most important point of your game! A well-chosen landing point can make or break the overall accuracy of your game.

Let me explain.

In any terrain there is always a chance of hitting a stone when your boule makes contact with the ground. Often the stone will result in your boule kicking off to one side. However, if you have succeeded in putting a back spin on your boule the chances of a diversion are greatly reduced by up to 80%.

How do you judge your landing point? It's a bit of a 'Chicken and egg' situation which is governed by the amount of distance you want your boule to 'roll out'.

For myself I always prefer to test a terrain with a half lob throw. That means if I want to send the boule out to approximately eight meters, then I will aim for a landing point approximately four meters down the terrain. For the sake of this example, let's say you 'lob' the boule to a height of 1.5 meters. If the boule only goes to the seven-meter mark, I now have a couple of choices. I can pick a new landing point at the distance of perhaps four and a half meters from the circle, or I can keep the same landing point and lob the boule to a little lower in height, so it rolls out a little further.

If the boule travels, after the first throw, to a distance of nine meters my choice is still two-fold in that I can either toss the boule to a higher level and maintain the same landing point. Alternatively, I can bring my landing point back towards the circle by a half meter.

There is no substitute for getting to a terrain a little early and throwing two or three boules to get an idea of how much rollout there is on a terrain. It only takes a minute to get a feel for the terrain.

Once you start the game, you have a few things to think about. Does the terrain slope towards either end? Is the stone surface fairly consistent or is it fairly patchy?

This might only work for me, but I do realise that the game will never be over in just a couple of ends. It will usually take anything up to twelve ends or more. So, if you stuff up on the first end and your throw goes way past the target. At the very worst, you can use it as a learning situation and realise that the terrain is possibly an 'intermittent' terrain. That means it has a differing layer of stones on the surface. If you have hit a fairly bald spot for stones, your boule will skate on past the Jack. If you hit a fairly thick layer of stones, then your boule will stop short by up to a meter short of the Jack. With the 'New way of aiming' you can now pick your preferred landing spot depending on the stone coverage you feel it has and any adjustment will be to the height of the lob with which you execute the throw.

Let's start at the beginning.

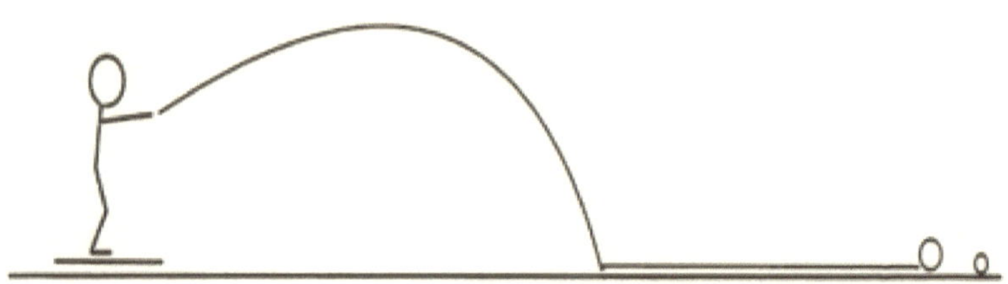

Diagram 4.4 shows the throwing position for the half lob throw.

You are standing behind the circle and lining up the edge of the circle with your target. That could be the Jack or a target boule. I have said before that the ideal way is to determine your landing point and let your brain work out how much 'lob' or height you need to put on the boule and how much you allow your boule to roll out before it stops. You have made this decision at least a thousand times before in your petanque games so don't get in the way of your brain.

For myself I can pick a landing point anywhere between forty percent of the distance to a point as far away as perhaps seventy five percent. This usually means I can pick out a landing point that is fairly smooth and consistent in its stone covering. So that is what I do! I am still stood behind the circle and eyeballing a line from the edge of the circle to whatever my target is.

Once I have determined my landing point, I make an adjustment to my stance so that once I enter the circle my right hand is well positioned <u>above the right-hand edge of the circle</u> and also my feet are well positioned in relation to the target line. I reacquaint myself with my proposed landing point and allow my brain a second or so to do whatever it wants to do in relation to the height I will send the boule. Then I send my boule on its way!

I love Mnemonics!

What I would like you to do before you step in the circle is repeat this Mnemonic

$$T\text{ -—}T/L\text{ —-}L/P$$

Which Stands for "Target -—Target Line -—Landing point."

Let's go over them.

Target -

The most important thing to do first is decide what actually is your target. We remember the image of the player standing in the circle. Think of this point. Their hand is probably over/hiding the jack (in relation to their aiming or dominant eye), and it is also covering at least another square foot of the target zone. When you get to the Gary Player story later in the book you will realise how he was so successful. For now, if you are content to accept a target zone that is at least a foot square, then you are already doomed to mediocrity! Your boule will most likely land, on average, within a couple of feet of the Jack (on a good day).

With the 'new way of aiming' you actually have the ability to get your boule to stop within an inch or two from the jack, or to hit the target boule if you are shooting. So, I ask you to have belief in yourself and reclassify your target. Do you want to land within a couple of inches from the jack or do you want to take out a target boule! Make the decision and that becomes the target!

We have already mentioned the (imaginary) line between the edge of the circle and the target (boule or Jack). Make sure, once you have decided on the target, that you can now see, in your mind's eye, a clear line between the right-hand edge of the circle and your intended target!

Target-Line

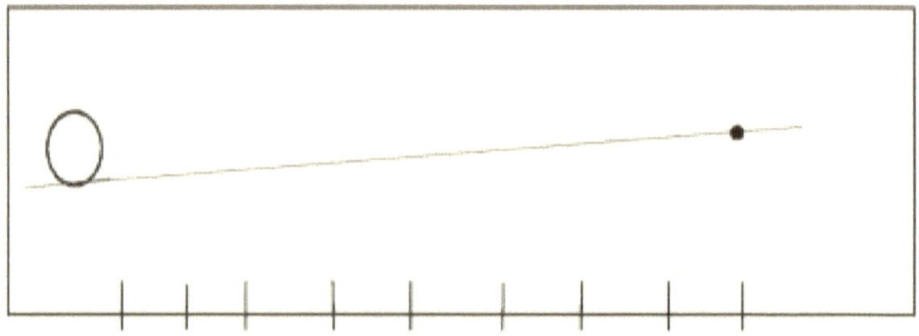

Diagram 4.2. Shows the "imaginary line" extending beyond the circle and the jack.

Landing Point –

I have already said that the landing point is the most important point in Petanque, and I stand by that point!

You have already worked out the specific target you want to hit (Boule or Jack). You already have the line you wish to use to get your boule towards it's intended target. The next thing is to work out your landing point on the target line. Your landing point is the great variable. And I could devote another chapter or so to how to pick your landing point, but it would be of no use whatsoever, because your landing point will differ from mine as I may well lob my boule to a different height than you do. All I can say is to get to the terrain a minute or so early and lob a few boules down to work out what works for you. As I said earlier, I try to get there early and try for a halfway landing point. Then I make the necessary adjustment of either distance or height that I lob the boule to.

The key thing I want you to take away from this section is the mnemonic of

T – T/L – L/P

If you remember this small thing it will help to lift your game to a much higher level!

As soon as the boule leaves my hand, <u>I have lost any and all control of its path</u>. Let's say that again. Once the boule has left my hand, I have lost all control of the boules final stopping point. Being aware of that point helps me to become more aware of where my boule landed. If you like I switch off from being a pointer and become an observer. I will check to see that my boule achieved its desired landing point and that my boule is still rolling out on a straight path. If it doesn't achieve the desired landing point, I will ask myself why? If the boule does not travel in a straight line, I will again ask myself why?

If the boule went well and either hit its target or landed close to the Jack, I will accept the plaudits of my teammates. If it missed for any reason, I want to know why! Did it hit a stone when it landed and that made it deviate onto a random path? That was simply unlucky, and I will pick a different landing point for my next boule. If it appears that I accidentally put a left- or right-hand curve on the boule, I will make the effort to ensure that doesn't happen again.

If the boule stopped short of the target, was there a patch of thick stone I didn't notice or did I just not pick the correct landing spot. If the boule went too far past the target, did I pick the wrong landing point or was there a bare patch of terrain that I did not notice, and the boule simply skidded on past the target.

For myself, and this is a personal feeling, if my first boule missed its intended target, I would sooner have another point, or shot, there and then so I can make any adjustment immediately while the first shot is fresh in my mind.

So many players (club players) I see have no idea of the importance of the landing point. They will stand in the circle with their arm extended, trying to get a read on the appropriate target and then fire the boule away in a state of optimism. If the boule misses its target, they have no idea of how to make a correction other than try the same method of aiming again.

If you spend a few minutes looking at the top players in our sport, I'll widen that by including the very good players in our sport, do not waste their time by trying aim at a boule. For the most part they will repair the divot where they wish to land (even if there is no divot there) and then hold the boule well below their eyeline while they allow the brain to work out line and pace etc. they have already worked out their landing point before they finally step into the circle. I've noticed a growing trend where the team will even decide on a landing point before the player steps into the circle. Watch the top teams. They will almost have a mini conference on where the previous boule landed and where the next boule should be aimed at as a landing point.

With the new method of aiming, you now have a pretty accurate way of aiming your boule and you are prioritizing the landing point rather than the intended target.

Trust me! It will pay dividends in terms of your results!

I attended a club day yesterday and it confirmed what I was saying earlier in this chapter. Probably, 70% or higher, of players focus only on the target and don't give a second thought to the landing point. It may be something I have always recognised but the landing point is the most important point of your game. Imagine, if you will, letting your boule land on a very stony patch of the terrain. By stony I mean having an area perhaps a foot or more in length that is covered by large and chunky stones. By recognizing this as an area where your boule is almost certain to kick away to the side, you can pick a different landing point that is relatively smooth and will afford your boule the chance to go forward in the manner you had hoped for.

What length do you 'lob' the boule to?

This should determine your landing point.

I do watch quite a bit of the top French players playing in their tourneys. And I am still amazed at how they react so nonchalantly to the boule that lands and kicks sideways at an alarming angle. Having said that I also have watched these same players play on a terrain that is so forgiving that they can almost bowl a boule along the entire length of the terrain. Technically there are, I suppose, three types of pointing throw. Plus, the "head-to-head" throw used for shooting.

- **The quarter lobs**.

Diagram 4.3 showing the amount of Lob' and Rollout for this point.

This is the pointing style where the boule lands less than a quarter of the way down the terrain and continues to roll on down the terrain to the head. To be honest, this is the shot most new players to the game use until they determine to become better players. Often the boule will travel to a height of no more than a meter. On a smooth and forgiving terrain, even the top players will use this shot. Given that the ends are often in the range of 8 to 10 meters, there is still quite a lot of skill in ensuring the boule travels the appropriate amount. The players may often crouch for this shot and the boule never gets more than a couple of feet off the ground.

As a coach I wouldn't suggest you persist with this type of pointing as there are so many better ways to devote your practice time towards.

- **<u>The half lobs</u>**.

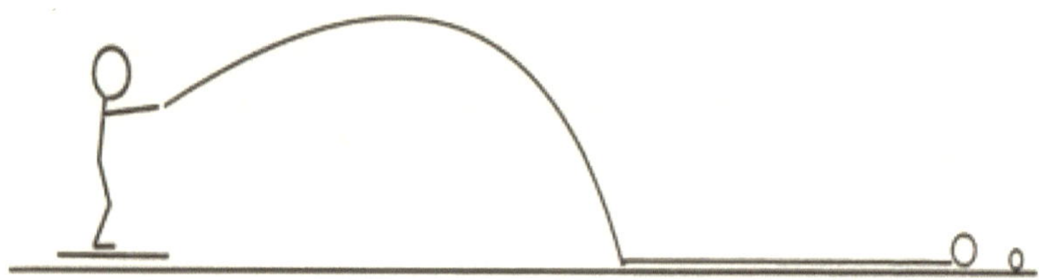

Diagram 4.4 showing the halfway style of lob.

Probably the most preferred shot by the average club player. As it is implied, the half lob shot requires the player to lob the boule approximately half of the distance and relies on the boule running for the rest of the way to the head. This boule is different in that, depending on the player and/or the length of the target, the boule can reach a height of between one and three meters high and the player will use either the standing position or the squatting position to play the boule.

This pointing style can be the easiest to vary in that the boule can be lobbed up to <u>three quarters</u> of the way to the head and the height of the lob will determine how much rollout occurs when the boule makes contact with the ground. This is also the easiest pointing style to make an adjustment on. If your first boule stops short of the head then your next boule should either be aimed at a landing point further away from the circle or, alternately, give the boule a little less height in the lob and keep approximately the same landing point so there is a little more rollout towards the head.

To practice this styles of pointing, get a couple of club members to hold a stick or broom at around 1 to 1.5 meters high and perhaps three of four meters away from the circle. Your role is toss the boule over the held out stick and to land it within a meter of the stick and then judge your rollout length. Have half a dozen attempts and make the adjustments to have a differing rollout length. Your next job is to get on one end of the stick while your club mate has a go at it.

- <u>**The three-quarter lob**</u>.

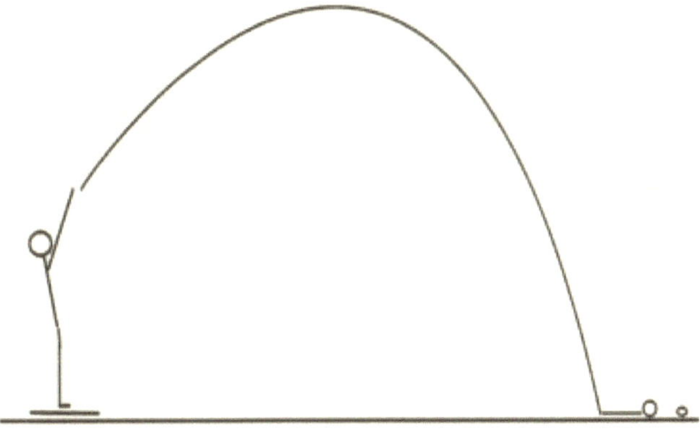

Diagram 4.4 showing the 'Plombee' style of pointing.

This is a slight misnomer as for the most part, the boule will travel to around 90% of the distance and will have relatively little rollout. Sometimes this shot is called the 'Plombee' (A euphemism for a lump of lead) as it goes up so high that it comes down nearly vertically, as in a lump of lead. Many of the top players will use this style of pointing shot for a difficult and unforgiving terrain. However, as a word of caution, I have seen a couple of players use this type of shot where the angle of the lob is so steep that the boule seems to come down almost vertically and will then bounce in any of the 360 degrees of direction available. If this happens, you have sent the boule too high for the distance you are trying to achieve. Or maybe you just got that one wrong!

This type of pointing style is not so difficult to pull off, with a little practice, but not many senior players can easily pull off the required effort to send the boule to its desired 3 to 5 meters in height.

To practice this style is not so difficult. Place a broom or rake on the ground at five or six meters from the circle. Lob the boule with sufficient height that it lands just beyond the marker and has a rollout that is less than a meter long. The length of rollout is the most crucial factor here and this length of lob is usually used for the most unforgiving terrains. If you are getting too much rollout, try lobbing the boule to a greater height. When you are getting a reasonable amount of success with the marker at the shorter distance, place the marker perhaps another meter away from the circle and try again.

The 'Head-to-head' Shot or shooting style.

Diagram 4.5 showing the 'tete a tete' (head-to-head) style of shooting.

This is the shot where you attempt to land your boule onto the target boule with a 'tete-a-tete', (head-to-head) action. Importantly, most users of this shot will attempt to put a low trajectory on this shot. The trajectory would probably not exceed 1.5 meters from the ground. The idea being that when the boule lands, the resulting low trajectory of the rebound means the boule will still have a low trajectory and will still hit the target.

When it does hit, it looks quite spectacular. When it misses the target, it looks like a complete failure and the boule you have thrown is soon going over the dead boule line into ignominy.

I get told quite often this is the most demanding type of shot, and it is! It commands accuracy of line and accuracy of length. So, let me make it a little easier for you. Let me explain. The boule is an average of 75 mm wide. If you get an overlap of the boule of, say, 10 mm it will still make the target boule move if you hit it with just a 10mm overlap between the two boules. So, you have a pocket of latitude perhaps 200mm wide (Three boules wide less two times the 10mm overlap which equals around 200mm wide) to still have an impact on the boule. In a forward to backward direction if you generally land your boule up to 150mm short and even as far forward as slightly past the vertical midpoint of the target boule, then you will still have an impact on the target boule.

So, you effectively have a target area of 200mm wide and a little over 200mm long. So, if you are standing in the circle and you have to throw a shooting boule head-to-head, you actually have a square target area of approximately 200mm wide by 200mm long. That's not far from the size of a dinner plate! That certainly seems a little less daunting than before. Don't get me wrong, I applaud those players who use this type of shot for shooting. I sometimes question the wisdom of using this shot when it is such a hit-or-miss in terms of the result.

I also wonder at the efficacy of this shot in comparison to a 'point with attitude' type of shot. In the next chapter of the book I go into the 'hit rate' of the variety of shooters in our game. It is an eyeopener!

How to practice this shot? Believe it or not I set the target boule at only three meters from the circle and hit it from the circle three times. Then I move the target boule perhaps another half meter from the circle and try to hit it again, three times from three.

One thing I have learned from being a coach is this. Never get into the habit of not being successful. If you straight away set your jack at the seven-meter mark and miss a few attempts, it only serves to reinforce a losing or failing mentality. I really do set the first boule in this practice at the three-meter mark so that I straight away get into a winning or success-based mentality.

Then I progressively move the target boule a half meter at a time further away from the circle and attempt to hit it three from three. When I get to six meters from the circle, I'm happy to hit it two times out of three. This style of shooting is not my preferred way of shooting. I'm getting far more accurate results with the "New way of aiming' and the 'Pointing with attitude;' style of shooting.

Here's another small trick I learned as a coach." Demand the best of yourself!"

By that I mean if you are trying for a 'head-to-head' shot you want to hit the target boule fully in the rear face, so that the target boule is moved forward and your boule will probably stay as a carreau! Accept it as a minor failure if you hit the target ten millimeters to the side of the centre line. The key thing is that you are trying to hit the target boule as accurately as you can, every time! Set yourself high standards as that is the best way to get better!

Probably, on the rare occasion when I need to use the 'head-to-head' style of shooting, it happens when I have to come over a boule that is in front of the target boule. Usually, before I resort to the 'head-to-head' style of shoot I would eliminate the possibility of using my preferred style of shooting by checking there is nothing that I could possibly promote forward to nudge the target boule out of the way. As I have said on many occasions in this book, this book is not for the top players in the world who are comfortable with a 'head-to-head' style of shooting. This is for the average club player who wants to get better. All I am trying to do here is to demystify what would seem like a very daunting shot. And if you have not already guessed it, my head-to-head shooting has a very poor success rate of less than 1 in 2 as it's now a shot I really don't practice or use that much.

(umpire question)

Team A throws the first boule thrown after the game starts.

Immediately, Team B shot their boule, and the two boules went out-of-bounds. There are no boules left on the terrain.

Which team should throw the boule next, A or B?

Chapter 5: Improving your pointing.

In the previous chapter we discussed the importance of your landing point. If you haven't quite understood it's importance, I'd strongly suggest you go back and re read Chapter 4.

So now we are able to get ourselves pointing in a straight line. What's next.

We are also now able to get a really obvious target line without all of the holding your hand out in front of your throwing shoulder. So, what comes next?

Obviously, we should now be able to work out our target line and also do a straight-line point, so we should be able to execute a straight-line point to our selected target!

The 'point' is the shot we have played the most often in our petanque lives so now we should be able to get that point leaving our hands with the reasonably confident expectation it will land within a few inches of our target line.

Let's set you up for that point.

First you will stand behind the right-hand edge of the throwing circle to work out your line to the target. The left-hand side for the left handed pointers.

Next you will work out approximately where you want your landing point to be. I'm going to suggest somewhere approximately halfway to your target.

Next you will walk up the terrain to the approximate area of your landing point and see if you still like that as your landing point. There may a be a divot to repair, so repair it, but do make a note of a nearby divot that you can uses as a reference point (e.g. your landing point is approximately three inches farther away and two inches to the right of the divot you now have as your marker reference.)

Walk back to the circle and stand with feet inside the circle. For myself, I always walk back past the circle, and recheck my line, so I can readily align my feet inside the circle in the correct position.

When I step in the circle, I know my feet are aligned correctly. I know my target line is spot on. I've already worked out my landing point. I look up and down the terrain to allow my brain to do what it wants to do and then I release the boule.

Obviously, I expect my boule to go within an inch or two of the intended target. Sometimes I may miss the target line by a couple of inches and because I know the intended landing point, I am already aware that the boule will miss. Sometimes I may hit the landing point and the boule misses because it deviated left or right. Check the divot, repair the divot and get on with your next throw.

Obviously, I am also expecting the boule to be close to the Jack. If it is not within a very close proximity to the Jack, I'd want to know why. If it went a half meter past the Jack, it's an indication my landing point was too far from the circle. Make the adjustment (bring your landing point closer to the circle by a half meter) and play your next boule accordingly. In a similar manner, if the boule landed a meter short of the Jack, then again, I would make the adjustment (move your landing point a half meter further from the circle) and play my next boule.

So, when you are picking your target line, where is the best line!

For myself (and everybody will be different) my ideal first point is straight in line with the Jack and around six inches short of the Jack. I do explain this later in the book so I will only briefly go into detail. If you are playing in either a club game or a tourney the shooter on the opposition team will not be that good on average! And most teams will have a couple of points at getting past your boule first. Because they are scared of giving your boule a nudge closer to the jack, they will usually give it a bit of space, so they won't generally be getting too close to your boule! If they get past your boule, their boule will most likely be up to eight inches away from the Jack, so you are still 'holding'.

What if you can't pick a target line in a direct line with the Jack? It happens! There may be a small pile of big stones on your preferred target line. But a boule within six inches of the Jack will still be a mental block for your opposition. Set your target line within an inch or so of the Jack and you will still be a worry to the opposition.

The last thing to cover in the talk about the landing point is how far down the terrain do you 'lob the boule' to, to make it land exactly next to the jack?

I don't know!

It's the million-dollar question.

Your lob may be to a differing height than mine.

Your terrain may have a differing amount of soft top surface than mine.

This is one of the things I cannot determine for you. To get the answer to this question you will have to turn up a few minutes early and throw a few boules down the terrain. Try using a longer or shorter lob. Try a higher or lower lob height. Understanding the dynamics of an individual terrain is very much a feel thing for every player. All I can tell you is that if you have the landing point and lob and the rollout under control and well-practiced, then no terrain should defeat you.

There is one other thing I cannot make a suggestion for. What is the right boule size for me?

In answering that question I'd want to know a few things about you first.

Are you a shooter?

Are you a pointer? Are you an all-rounder (or Milieu)

What I'm about to add is a very generalized comment about the boules I would recommend

If you are a shooter, you should probably use a lighter boule (660 to 690 Gram) Steel or carbon is irrelevant and comes down to personal choice. I would however suggest a boule with fewer markings or striations. The main reason for this is that you want the boule to be disturbed minimally by the surface of the terrain.

If you are a Pointer, I would recommend a boule in the range of 670-700 gram weight. Most pointers would prefer a boule with more striations than a shooter. My wife recently purchased a set of MS Boules that look similar to a grenade (CZ Inox). Okay for Pointing but not so enjoyable for shooting as the extreme striations tend to be influenced by every stone. She is not comfortable with their feel when she shoots so I can imagine we'll be looking at the Boules catalogue again.

For the allrounder (Milieu) I'd suggest a boule with similar pattern to a shooter with less striations. I have recently purchased a set of Obut boules with a quarter pattern on them. I believe they are called 'Strie 2' which I am enjoying playing with and I'd call myself an allrounder.

As to which size boule you should play with, I'd strongly suggest that you play a game with a set of boules to get a feel for them. Borrow a set from another player to try them out. For myself I always felt comfortable with 72 mm boules so that was one decision less I had to make when purchasing new boules.

Umpire Question

Team A throws the jack and it is just under the 6.00 meter mark by twenty centimeters. Team B say they are quite happy to play the jack as it lies. Can they do this?

Chapter 6: Point with attitude!

I've mentioned a couple of times before that the shooter is the one player who has an instant verdict on whether their shot was successful. They either hit the target or they miss the target! I might be quite hard on this shot. I count the boule as successful if it achieves the desired result and the target boule is removed or one of your own boules becomes the holding boule! If a shooter misses the target and takes out the Jack by accident, to me that is a failed shot as they missed their target boule. It might be a lucky result, it might be a fluke, but to me it is still a fail! In most circumstances their boule will now be at the far end of the terrain, or over the dead ball line. Either way, their boule is very unlikely to be among the boules that will be measured at the completion of the end. And if they only 'winged the target boule' then I still struggle to count that as a successful shot. If it didn't work, it's a fail!

As an aside, the shooter who has too heavy a boule will struggle because of the sheer tiredness of your throwing arm at the end of a day's play. It's a generally accepted axiom that a shooters boule will weigh less than 700 grams. The lighter boule is also much easier to aim. It's a personal thing only but my shooting has improved when I started using the lighter weighted boules.

Right, where were we?

Oh yes, we were talking about the shooting aspect of the game. If only there was a way that the shooter could end up with an even chance of their boule being a 'counter'.

Oh, wait! There is a way.

Before I go into this new method let me just explain a few things about shooting.

The **average** shooter will only hit the target once every two attempts. Really? Yep, and that is why they really are average.

Look at the table below.

Rocher/Fazzino / Rizzi Suchaud/ Quintais/ Pucchinelli etc	These are the top shooters in our sport. Predominantly French or Italian	Likely to hit 80% of the time	Success rate 4 out of 5
Second tier shooters such as Lacroix or Robineau or Malbec	Usually on the professional level and playing in Europe	Likely to hit three quarters of the time	Success rate 2 out of 4
Your top local shooters	Regional shooters on the tourney circuit.	Success rate 50% Occasionally 66%	Likely to hit 1 out of 2 (on a good day 2 out of 3)
Your average club shooter	Club players	Success rate 33%	Likely to hit 1 out of 3
Normal club shooter	Fancies themselves as an occasional shooter	Success rate 25%	Likely to hit 1 out of 4
The last player of the end who is encouraged to give it a shot to perhaps get 3 points	Likes to think of themselves as a pointer but easily encouraged to 'give it a go'	Success rate 10%	Likely to hit 1 in 10

Diagram 6.1 showing the relative accuracy of the shooters you may come across.

Okay, surely these players are better than that? Well, they may be for one game. But over a day of play, or a weekend? I have spent enough time as an umpire to sit back and watch these players, even at a national championship level or on the professional French tour (on TV), and the above statistics are pretty much spot on. To watch the top players, sign into YouTube and enter the word Petanque. To watch the second or third tier players, sign into YouTube and use the search word for Petanque and add your country name to the search term.

When I was a more prolific shooter and getting in lots of practice, I'd like to think I occasionally got into the third-tier level of hitting 2 out of 3. The reality is, for the most part, I was probably hitting 1 out of 2. I also considered myself to be reasonably successful on the competition circuit.

So, when you watch a shooter at a local club level, don't be so afraid they are going to knock your boule out, just because they step into the circle. The reality is more likely that they will only hit 1 shot in 3 or 1 in 4.

Right, back to reality.

The new way I have started to Shoot is called" Pointing with Attitude".

It's a phrase I devised when I was playing as an invited third player into an established doubles team. The shooter of the duo was one of the old-fashioned style of players who had a tendency to hurl his boule at the target. He was missing more than 75% of the time and costing us the game. Also, his boules were mostly going out over the dead ball line. I used my 'pointing with attitude' to good effect and we won about half of our games. I had an issue of not stepping on this guy's ego as they were a regular doubles combo. I watched a video of this same guy playing in a tourney a couple of weeks ago and he is still hurling the boule down the terrain and still only achieving a hit rate of around

25%. His partner is quite an accurate pointer which is a shame as his shooting lets the team down, I feel.

Okay, so here it is. The entire secret to <u>pointing with attitude</u> is this. If you want to move an opposing boule which is, say seven meters away, you shoot the boule, but you only use enough velocity on your boule so that if it misses, <u>your boule will only go 8 meters</u>. If you hit the target boule, your boule should stay (and be holding) and the target boule is now probably up to a meter away from the Jack!

Imagine the following scenario. You are standing in the circle. The opposition is holding the point and about six inches in front.

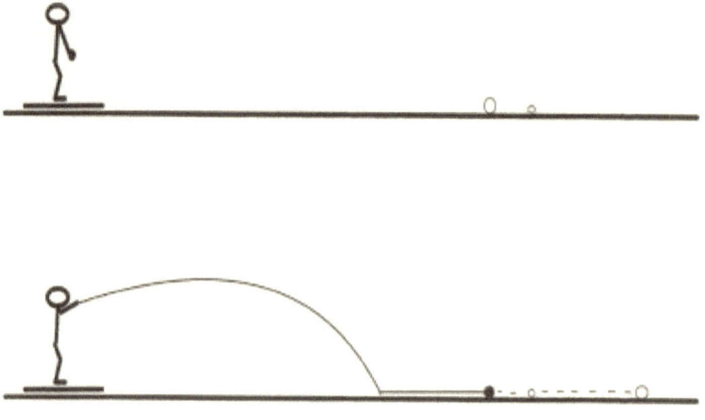

Diagram 6.2 & 6.3. Above scenario. Target boule replaced with own boule and now you are holding the point!

I admit, there is a little more to it than that. But the basic premise is still the same. The key thing to remember is that you don't shoot with more velocity than to go a *maximum* of a meter beyond the target boule!

Why is this revolutionary?

Firstly, we are now shooting (pointing with attitude) with an accuracy we had never achieved before!

Secondly, if you think about it, at our standard of game there are often 6 or 8 boules around the Jack when it is time to measure for points. We have already noted that in the top level of the game there may only be 2 or 3 boules within a meter of the Jack. Already, with our type of game, we have way more boules that could be considered for points.

- If we inadvertently move our own boule, it is still within the '1 meter circle' and may still count.
- If we only disturb the boules within a 1-meter circle, there is every chance we won't do too much damage to the head. This is in preference to hurling a boule down that clears away everything in its path, usually one of our own boules if the shooter is a bit wild with their aim.
- And, last but not least, importantly! When we aim a boule to only go six or seven or eight meters, there is a degree of finesse about the point. Compare that to the hurling down of a boule that is destined to go over the dead boule line.
- Let's just go over the last point I made. When you are trying to hurl down a boule to take out a point at seven meters you are still hurling that boule down with sufficient pace on it for the boule to go over the dead boule line! You have hurled that boule down the terrain at full force to make the target boule move. You have to admit that if you are only throwing your boule to go eight meters (target boule is seven meters plus one meter of 'attitude') there is an unbelievable amount more of finesse in your delivery! Also, if you think about it, when you move one of your own boules accidentally by hitting it, the boule will still move up to a meter away with the less force boule.

Make no mistake, we are only pointing the boule (with a little attitude) so there is usually far more control involved.

Now this technique goes hand in hand with the previous chapter (a new way of pointing). For myself, I have proved countless times the 'new way of aiming' and the 'pointing with attitude' and I'd appreciate if you would give my methods a try. The only thing you have to lose is being called an average player.......

To practice this technique is not too complicated. Put a boule on the terrain at six meters and another boule at seven meters. Your landing spot is around halfway (three to three and a half meters) for this exercise. Point your boule so that it goes past the six-meter mark but not past the seven-meter mark. In theory you wish to hit the boule at six meters, but your boule should not go past the boule at the seven-meter mark. When you are happy you have this down, put the boule at six meters out to the eight-meter mark. Now you point the boule, so it goes past the seven-meter mark but not the eight-meter mark. Carry on doing this exercise to the nine- and ten-meter mark until you feel confident you have the control in your pointing. Now repeat the exercise by placing the boule at the six-meter mark in the centre of the terrain. Point (with attitude) to not beyond the seven-meter mark and try to take out, or nudge, the boule at six meters. If you are pointing in a straight line, it should not be a major obstacle to hit the six-meter boule. This technique, of course, is to be used in conjunction the 'New way of Aiming' technique if you want your game to raise itself to the next level. This exercise is also a great way of picking out your landing point(s).

See Diagram 6.1 & 6.2 above.

I recently ran a coaching clinic and it occurred to me that I now have three methods of shooting a target boule.

- Method 1: is the original <u>head-to-head</u> (tete-a-tete) style of shooting. This is where you send your boule down with quite some velocity to clear the target boule away from the head.
- Method 2: <u>point with attitude</u>. This is where you send the boule to a landing point around halfway down the terrain and only with sufficient velocity to go no more than one meter past the target.
- Method 3: is the <u>modified shooting</u> method, where the landing point of the boule is around 75% of the distance to the target and the boule is launched with just a little more attitude than the 'pointing with attitude' type of shot. This is used more often when the target boule wants to be moved with more force but there is still a good chance of a 'carreau' with a good contact.

Could you be an umpire?

Players are not allowed to smoke or drink alcohol etc during a game. What about a player eating some food? Is that permitted under the rules?

Chapter 7: The Umpire is your friend.

I was going to conclude the book with comments about Tips, hints, tactics and observations.

But I didn't realise I would have so many tips and observations etc.

Let's try and get organised. For this chapter, I have my umpire's hat on.

Okay, right up front let me say this:

The Umpire is your friend!!

I really mean that. If you generally obey the rules or look like you are that type of player, then the umpire is your friend. It's a little like the speeder on the road who always wants to drive ten or more above the speed limit. If you are that type of driver who drives without regard for other road users, then the police will be your enemy and you will see them as a killjoy. In a similar manner the petanque player who chooses to ignore certain rules because they are perceived to be 'fun limiting' or 'too technical' or (my favourite) "It's only a game, why do we need all these rules?" is also not going to like the umpire who pulls them up.

The rules are there to make the game safe and fair for all players. So, the bullies on the terrain will not overpower the gentler players by dubious tactics or power plays. My suggestion to you is that you read and understand the rules so that you don't run afoul of them. Speak to the umpires and be respectful to them. If you have a query or you don't like or understand some rule interpretation by an opponent, then be sure and call the umpire over to get a clearer interpretation by the only person whose decision will actually matter. Let me also say there are umpires who are well versed with the rules of the game and there are also the other kind! I strongly feel there should be refresher courses for umpires at least once yearly as a precursor to getting their umpire license renewed. As an umpire, we are strongly discouraged to make comments about other umpires' interpretations of the rules so I will only admit there are some umpires who make more of an effort to be completely up to date with the rules and leave it at that. There is usually a network among the local umpires who discuss new rulings etc, so every umpire is up to date if they wish to be. On a personal level there are also internationally ranked umpires who operate Facebook pages where umpires can ask the opinion of a very senior umpire. For myself, I am particularly grateful to Mike Pegg (The senior UK umpire) and Andre Deramond (The senior Oceania umpire) for the effort they put into their replies to all of the questions they receive.

Many players have a somewhat distorted view or interpretation of the rules. Let me be generous and say these players have probably been the recipient of somebody else pushing the rules down their throat, so don't be too harsh. Among the more stupid rules I have been presented with is the one that the player confidently asserts that 'no player is allowed to kill the end on the last end of a timed game.' Well in actual fact that is not the case. When an end is killed in the final end of a timed game, the result still stands, and the score will reflect the situation at the completion of that timed end. However, if the score is tied *after* that final end, then another end is played and if the Jack is killed, the jack is replaced (and the Jack MUST be marked). For more details of that rule, please take a second and read that particular rule (article 21). It really is not complicated, but it is a rule that keeps cropping up by misinformed players. Another 'Rule' I came across this weekend is a player who queried my moving the circle back to around nine meters from the far end of the terrain. He knew beyond doubt that a player could only move the circle a maximum of two paces from where it originally sat. Yeah, we got the rules out and came to a compromise. He admitted I was correct! That's the kind of compromise I like.

Later in the book I have added a full chapter with the Rules of Petanque and added some comments. For now, I just want to put some tips in place for you, relating to the rules.

Anticipate some quiet when you are in the circle.

If your opponent is not behaving when you are in the circle, call the umpire over. You are entitled to the same amount of quiet that you afford to the opponent when they are in the circle. Don't be timid in turning around and asking them to shut up! If they are talking loudly enough to be heard by you when you are in the circle, they are affecting your concentration on your shot. If they are persistent in their chatter, get the umpire involved! You aren't being a killjoy because they don't know or choose to ignore the rules!

"We're holding!"

If your opponent has a habit of swiftly looking at the head and stating, "That's ours", and you disagree or are a little uncertain, don't be bullied by them! Whoever threw the last boule played is the team that should be doing the measuring. Don't be afraid to ask them to measure accurately and if you are still not happy, Ask the umpire to come over and measure. It's a personal opinion on my part, but I believe that many players are too quick to give away the point because their opponent is perceived to have vastly more experience. Also, if you are on the receiving end of such a trick, the very fact that you queried their assertion will make them a little more hesitant to try the same trick again. Note I stated in this paragraph that it is the responsibility of the team that threw the last boule to do the measure. Do not volunteer to do the measuring for them! By all means lend them your measure if they don't have one (which they should). Partly, it shows them you are not to be bullied by them. More importantly, if during the measure you move a boule or the Jack, you are the player penalized by losing that point. That will hurt, especially if you have done them the favour by measuring for them. And one more thing I have fallen foul of! Don't be the gentleman who offers to get down to measure because the opposition is a bunch of little old ladies. They are the quickest to scream about it being their point, if you accidentally move the Jack or a boule!

Oh, and while I'm on the subject of measuring, any boule lifted off the ground before the points are agreed by *both teams* is automatically excluded from the count of points. It's right there in the rules. So, if a player rather quickly picks up one boule and then starts looking to which boule is next, that boule, if you haven't agreed it was holding, is now a dead boule and will not count. The umpire will only make a call on the situation at the head when they arrive. If a player quickly picks up, say, three boules without you agreeing, those boules are also all dead boules!

Let me list the most common things you might get a yellow card for.

I should add here for information purposes that the yellow and orange cards do not generally accumulate over a tournament. So, you may get a yellow card for an infringement on your first game, but if you get pinged again in game two, you will only get another yellow card. However, if you get a yellow card in game one and then the umpire sees the need to issue another warning in the same game, the card you receive should be an orange card with the resultant disqualification of a boule. For information on red cards look at the appropriate section in the chapter about the rules.

The major exception to this rule is the circumstance of a player behaving inappropriately towards another player or official etc. If this players behavior warrants the issue of a yellow card, then that yellow card remains in place for the <u>entire</u> tournament. A repetition of similar behavior can result in the next card issued for the offending player being a red card and the player is then disqualified for the rest of the tournament. This red card can be issued to the whole of the team should their actions warrant such a move. It is not a decision taken lightly by the umpire but if the players behavior is sufficiently bad, then the umpire should take whatever action they feel necessary to maintain the safety or dignity of all fellow players and officials and organizers. I have been the victim of such a display when I asked a player to vacate the terrain as he was smoking, and the start bell had rung. He went ballistic and turned violent. It turned out he had been on the booze all night and had come to the terrain straight from his boozing. This was in the days before yellow cards had been invented. Fortunately, there were sufficient players handy who witnessed the event and persuaded the player to vacate the terrain.

Also note that the umpire is expected to make a report on each tournament they officiate at and note any player they have carded. If the governing body takes a note that a player is a persistent offender from one tournament to the next, they can take the decision to bar that player for a period. Don't be the persistent offender!

Taking longer than one minute to throw the Jack or your next boule.

And there is a small trap here for the players. If the team takes longer than a minute to throw the Jack or a boule, be aware that the *entire team* is yellow carded. This is not a big deal in itself, but what if one team member receives another warning? The resultant next card turns into an orange card and one of the players boules is confiscated. It gets worse. If the *team* is awarded another warning for slow play, The *entire team* will be issued an orange card. Again, it is a team warning and the whole team will get a boule disqualified for each team member. Slow play is to be avoided.

I've now seen it on the TV. In a triples match between Rocher and Andriasahanto. The pre story requires some info. At 3-1 Andriasahanto team were given a yellow card for taking over the one minute for their shot. Of course, all the team received the yellow card as per the rules. When the score was 10-1 to Rocher. One of the Andriasahanto team took over the minute for their shot. Rocher was holding one point about a meter away from the jack. and they had three boules left to play, as did the Andriasahanto team. The shooter missed their shot but still took over the minute. The umpire walked on and lifted the boule that Andriasahanto team had played and then turned to the two other players on the team to take one of their boules as their forfeit. Despite their protests the team still had to forgo their boules, meaning that Team Rocher had three boules in hand and were already holding one point and leading 10-1 on the scoreboard. The Andriasahanto team turned around and congratulated the Rocher team as the result was inevitable. For me, the Umpire was correct in his decision making and on this rare occasion actually had the guts to do the right thing!

Not marking the circle

The player who threw the Jack is the player held responsible for marking the circle. That is the player that gets the warning.

Not marking the Jack

This is a trickier one to police. Although it is acknowledged the Jack must be marked and re-marked every time it is moved, the rules don't stipulate who exactly should mark the Jack. It is a general consensus among umpires that the person who threw the boule that moved the Jack is the player who gets the warning.

Standing 'not beyond the head or behind the throwing circle.'

Believe it or not, it is disturbing to the player in the circle to have a line of players between themselves and the Jack. Even if you are standing a few feet to the side on a spare terrain, you should still stand beyond the head or behind the circle. Also, be considerate and try to avoid your shadows impinging on the terrain. If you do it first, they may feel obliged to reciprocate.

Not keeping quiet or still when a player is in the circle and about to take their throw.

Worst experience is when the players are standing behind you when you are in the circle, and they don't shut up! Next worst experience is when you are readying to take your shot and the players at the far end of the terrain are either continuing to talk or moving around. Correction, the next worse situation might be when one or more players is standing right beyond the Jack you are throwing to. To be fair, this type of offence is usually committed through ignorance of lack of forethought and is rarely a deliberate ploy to disturb the player in the circle.

Gardening

It's a phrase used by umpires when a player is considered to be overly zealous when repairing a divot. Usually, they sweep their foot over a space that is considerably more than the size of a normal divot. That often means it's three or four or ten times the size of a normal divot. Sadly, the players at the very top of the game seem to get away with this behaviour which makes it harder for the umpires to police it a local level.

Practicing on an adjacent terrain

I really don't know why we get players committing this offence. Everybody knows you cannot do it! Yet we umpires still find ourselves showing a card for this. The rule is quite simple. You cannot practice your throw on an adjacent (or on the same) terrain while you are in the middle of a game. Even if you are between ends, you are still liable to get a card of some color. I know that the players on the top French circuits get away with a lot, which makes it hard for the local umpires to issue a card, but a local umpire who is not afraid of incurring the players wrath will readily get a card out and will quickly earn the respect of all the players on the terrain.

Smoking or vaping on the terrain.

For myself I still hark back to the old days when you could smoke or have a wine while you played. It's probably one of the things that attracted me to the sport, it's relaxed nature. However, the Smoking police and the Drinking police and the OSH teams have all got together and decided they know what is best for you, so nowadays, it is not allowed to happen that you smoke or drink or vape on the terrain. For me it's a slightly backward step but we do cater for all types on the terrain, so they are a no-go, and you will get a card for committing any of these offences. Generally during a competition, smoking/vaping/ drinking is a no go on the terrain. You can only do the above off the terrain and not during a game! However, during a game you are also not allowed to step off the terrain for a Smoke/vape or drink of alcohol. You have been warned! And the same restriction applies to using your mobile phone during a game. This includes the listening to music through ear pods etc. Listening to Music through ear pods etc is a clear safety issue as you cannot be made aware of your surroundings. Generally, not using your mobile phone is a nod to the others in the game that you are focused on the game in hand.

Standing on the edge of the circle.

It's always a no-no. However, there is another quirk to this rule that players are not often aware of. It is this. If you are crouching in the circle to make your shot, it is allowed for the player to have the raised part of their feet over the edge of the circle. However, if your feet drop back and touch the circle *before the boule has landed* you are deemed to have committed an offence. Also, if one of your feet leave the ground before the boule has landed, that is also an offence that will warrant a warning and card.

Touching the ground outside the circle.

This is an offence that is often overlooked but let me explain. When you are in the circle. It is permissible to touch the ground with your boule while you steady yourself. However, I recently watched a game on You Tube where Rocher was in a singles match against Fazzino. After throwing his boule Fazzino touched the ground, outside of the circle, to steady himself. The umpire was straight in with an orange card and Fazzino had his last-played boule lifted and removed. As only Fazzino can, he did register his polite protest, but the card still stood. Both Rocher and Fazzino were grinning at the umpires perhaps overzealous approach, but Fazzino still played that end with only two boules.

Leaving the terrain without permission.

It's a tricky one to police but the umpires are still obliged to do it. If there are two or more umpires at a tournament, you must ask the umpires permission to leave the terrain. If there is only one umpire for the tournament you need only ask the opposing players permission. I'm adding an extra into this ruling because it does happen, more than you might think.

In a timed game you obviously still ask the umpire or the opposition if there is only one umpire. Yes, we already know that! Here is the twist, in a timed game *you must also have played your boules before you can leave the terrain!*

If you have not played your boules before you leave the terrain, you are excluded from returning to the terrain until that end is complete. And your teammates are not allowed to play your boules on your behalf. Trust me, it is all there in the rules and it is designed so that the timed games will not be hindered by a player taking breaks and delaying the game unfairly. Timed games seem to be coming more of a thing in New Zealand as it allows the organizers to plan a little more clarity into their timetable. As a player you should be aware of the rules applicable to a timed game and act accordingly.

If I had the power to take a rule out or add a rule in, it would this one!

There is nowhere in the rules that stipulates who has to mark the new position of the Jack when it is moved. I would like for the next set of rules to add the following

"The player that throws the last boule when a Jack is moved has the responsibility to re-mark the Jack in its new position. Failure to do so will result in a warning. It is permitted for a team member to re-mark the Jack but it is the responsibility of the player that threw the boule that moved the Jack to its new position."

Currently there is a strong requirement to mark the new position of the Jack but nowhere in the rules does it state which player is actually responsible. For an umpire, marking the Jack is an important part of measuring. It seems only right that someone should be pinged for the offence. All I'm doing is nominating a player whose responsibility it would be.

Could you be an umpire?

This is a tricky one that happened when I was an umpire. Team A threw their first boule. Team B threw their first boule. Team A Captain who was standing by the head indicated that team B were holding and gestured to his team mate to throw the next boule. Team A threw all of their five remaining boules without disturbing the Jack or the two initial boules that were thrown. Team B then threw their five remaining boules, again without disturbing the Jack or the two initial boules thrown.

When the team captain of Team A looked again at the head, he decided to measure the boules and as a result awarded one point to team A.

I was stood on the footpath by the terrain, so I had a very good view of the complete end.

How would you have handled it?

Chapter 8: TACTICS and Observations, hints & tricks.

There is money in them there French terrains!

Just doing minimal research on the internet will reveal the following. Phillippe Quintais has a net worth of over 1.5 million Euros. Predominantly from his Petanque earnings and his sponsorship deals. I would imagine Phillippe Suchaud and Dylan Rocher will soon surpass that total.

The Marseillaise tournament attracts an average field of over 13000 players who each pay an entry fee of 24 Euros. Add that to the sponsorship deals the Tournament attracts and the money for the TV coverage etc and the total income for the tournament is well in excess of an anticipated 500,000 euros. Add to that an average of 200,000 paying spectators over the five days and you can imagine it is a sizeable revenue earner! So, when we hear that the average prize for winning the tourney is around 25000 Euros, we begin to realise how much of a spectator sport Petanque is in France. There are big tournaments most weekends in France and for the colder climes there are also the indoor terrains (boulodromes). Believe me when I say the top-level professionals are mostly making a good living on the top ranked tournaments.

Pointing. Stand up or squat in the circle.

For myself it doesn't really make that much difference. For a couple of years, I always adopted the squatting posture when I pointed. I liked to think that it gave me a much better view of the undulations of the terrain. I probably did it because I had seen the top players use the squatting position, and listened to their advice about the undulations etc. Ten years later I never use the squatting position. As I got a little older, I found it was getting more difficult to get up and down and, at the end of the day, my legs were beginning to refuse to cooperate. Now, with hindsight, I guess it doesn't really matter whether I stand or adopt the squatting posture. And it really shouldn't matter that much to you as a player. Do what you enjoy and whatever makes you feel comfortable. Please don't misunderstand me. I'm sure that those players who do adopt the squatting posture are quite confident they do get a benefit from this practice. It now no longer suits my style, and I don't feel I am losing too much by standing in the circle. I might take that one point further and add, in my own humble opinion, many players would be better off adopting the standing position for the longer shots or points. It would certainly give them a better view of the overall terrain and the decreased angle of attack would make the resulting rollout a little more predictable.

The one-minute rule

It's fairly clear in its wording. The team that won the point in the previous end, or the team that won the toss, has no more than a minute to toss out the Jack. Consensus of opinion seems to be that the minute starts *after* the points have been decided after the previous end. If there is a measure required, the clock is stopped (I should say the clock is only paused!). There is no time limit on how long a measure should take but if your opposition is taking a bit too much time, I'd suggest you call the umpire over to 'assist'. A couple of refinements to be aware of. Even if the newly thrown Jack is invalid that still counts as the Jack having been thrown and the next minute has started for the opposition to place the jack. As a technical issue, the minute starts when the jack has stopped rolling.

The second thing to be aware of is that if the opposing team place the Jack in an invalid position, the player that placed the Jack is liable for a warning (card), but that players team still retain the right to place the Jack in a valid position.

Fill your divot properly.

This a bugbear for me, as a coach. I know there are all sorts of ramifications for those players who are generous in their interpretation of what 'repairing a divot' actually means. Equally frustrating for me as a coach are those players who half fill a divot. They don't actually repair the divot but feel they should be doing some kind of divot repair because 'Well that's what the big players do.' If, by some freak chance that they actually land in this 'repaired' divot there is every chance their boule will skid off to one side because of the way they have repaired the divot. Please do this! Sweep the accumulated debris from *both* sides of the divot, that's two actions of the foot, and then gently tamp down the divot so the ground becomes relatively flat and smooth. I have been approached by an umpire who said it was illegal to actually 'tamp down' a divot. When I asked him to point out that particular infringement in the rules. He muttered something about it being a rule and said he would check it out. I have still to hear from the umpire about this and it has been over two years, so you work that one out.

And while we are on the subject of repairing the divot, be aware that the top players do not often repair a divot they think may be in their way. Most of the top players will walk up to the head and then smooth out the ground which they hope to use as their landing point. Watch them! It does kind of make sense, doesn't it?

Do you actually need to repair a divot?

I've stated once or twice that most players repair a divot and then miss the repaired divot by a foot or more. So, basically you are repairing the selected divot for the other players to appreciate? If you have decided where your landing point is going to be and you don't actually need to repair a divot, think about not repairing a divot that will usually only benefit your opponents.

If they put the boule long and left, you put it short and right!

When the player that throws the Jack out puts it out of the terrain or beyond the dead boule line. I ask you to think why they threw it in that position in the first place.

There are usually three reasons why the Jack is thrown to an invalid length.

1, The player that threw the Jack is a lousy thrower.

2, More likely is that the opposing team prefer to point to a long end or a short end

3. Even more likely, is that they have heard one of your team bemoan the fact that they don't like long ends (or short ends or being so close to the stringline etc) so they have tossed the Jack to a length that disadvantages your team.

It's a personal opinion only, but if the opposing team throws the Jack out long and left for whatever reason, when it becomes your team's opportunity to place the Jack, then you might consider placing it short and to the right. A Short and left position by your opponent's means you might consider placing the Jack in a longer and right-side position. It might get you into a position where you break their streak.

Know the rules.

I've also mentioned this before. There are so many players who believe they 'know' the rules and are quick to demonstrate their superior knowledge. For the most part, those players are not always right in their interpretations. As a recommendation, you should read the rules and have a reasonably good working knowledge of them. If there are any doubts about the rules, call an umpire over and let them decide if you are correct.

I am going to take that point a little further. You should reread the rules regularly. I'm not sure if that means you should read them once a month. For myself, I'd look through the rules around once a month and that helps me as an umpire. That is over to you. But a regular read of the rules may help you more than you think.

Use the forward spin throw for long distances.

This also happens more often than you might think. The Jack is displaced to beyond the ten-meter mark. As an avid student of the rules, you do know the Jack is still valid up to twenty meters away from the circle on an open terrain. How to throw to the Jack which is now maybe twelve or more meters away? It is not actually that difficult. Most petanque social players are getting on in years. They often struggle to get the boule out to ten meters with any degree of control. And even then, it is often a ball hurled down, with little finesse and more dependent on how far they can throw the boule. Here is a very simple trick to get the extra distance. Throw the boule so that you actually put *forward spin* on it.

Under normal circumstances we would try and put back spin on every boule we send down. At its best, we know that putting back spin on the boule gives us some feeling of control. Instead of summoning every ounce of strength you can muster into sending the boule to twelve meters, simply hold your palm in the palm-up position. It's an amazing amount less effort to get the boule to a greater distance. It's also seeming to be a lot easier to aim the boule over that distance. As I have said before, when you 'hurl' the boule down the terrain you lose quite a bit of control. Using this method makes it easier to retain some control and finesse. I'd say it is fairly easy to toss a boule to 15 or more meters away using this technique of applying forward spin, so it's something you might spend a little time practicing. This is only a guideline, but I'd suggest you try for a landing point around the quarter to one-third length as the forward spin boule will travel quite a bit further than you think. It's definitely worth ten minutes of your practice time!

Team tactics.

Whether you are a team of doubles or triples, you should have tactics.

For myself I always have a failure point. Let me explain. I will usually only allow two wasted boules out of the six boules we have available before I call a quick team conference.

What is a wasted boule? A wasted boule is a boule that was shot and missed its target and is now whiling away it's life on or near the dead boule line. Or it's a point that, for whatever reason, went past the Jack and carried on for another meter or so.

Once we have sent down two wasted boules it is time for a team talk to decide whether we risk another wasted boule or whether we decide right now to shut the head down by crowding the Jack and making it difficult for the opposition to get more than one point on that end. Often the team talk may result in deciding to potentially have another shot, but it does often depend on the caliber of your opponent.

For the average team playing another average team, there is little chance that your opponents will have a top shooter in their team who will remove everything you can put forward. Even if they have a good shooter, that player will only have two boules at their disposal (triples) or three boules (doubles.) so be aware that in the team talk you should be aware of the quality and quantity of the team you are playing against.

Have your team talk. Decide how many boules each player on your opposition has still to play and then decide whether to risk another shot or to try and contain the damage.

One interesting tactic I learned at the weekend is that many of the top teams will have a designated player whose side role is to keep a count of how many boules your opponents have still to play. I hadn't been aware of that. It seems that if you keep your ears open you can still learn. I'd like to take this a step further. How would it be if your shooter kept an eye on the opposition shooter, the pointer kept an eye on the pointer and the milieu kept an eye on the milieu. Firstly, they know how many boules the opposition player has played. They also can keep an eye on how they are doing. So, when you get your team talk going, they could say 'the Shooter has played two and he's only hit one. I think he is going to be pushed down and the milieu will be the shooter', 'the Pointer has only played one and is playing well'. 'The milieu has shot one and missed'. If you now realise, as captain, that you have four boules left to their two boules, it should make you rearrange your tactics, perhaps.

As an aside, the best shooters in your region or country will play well below their usual level when they are up against the best shooters in the world. If the opposition are playing well and on top of their game, it's usually because they don't fear you as a team!

I'm a right handed player, I don't like sending my boules along the left hand side of the head

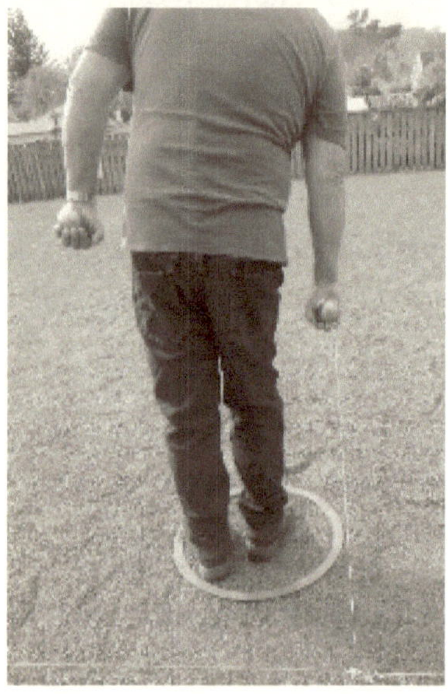

Diagram 8.1 & 8.2 showing the relative feet positions for a point on the right hand string line and 8.2 shows the feet position for a point on the left hand string line.

This is showing the stance/foot angle to throw a boule along the string line. The right-hand pic shows the clearly different stance to throw the boule to the left-hand string line. Note the clear difference in the stance and angle of the leading foot.

This is actually quite a common occurrence, and it is so easy to fix. Step to the rear of the circle, perhaps a couple of paces. Now line up your throwing arm with the side of the circle and the target boule or Jack. You need to adjust your feet to line up with this new direction. Now walk back into the circle and you are now automatically lined up with the direction of throw with your preferred (right) arm. Now pick your preferred landing spot and deliver the boule to the correct side.

Try not to accelerate your throwing arm from a stationary start!

There is a longer version of that title but let me explain it this way.

I suppose this is linked to those players who let the boule hang in a vertical position and then accelerate their arms from zero to a release. These players will usually attempt a 'Plombee' Type of shot. So here is something for those players to think about.

Diagram 8.3 shows the 'bent-arm' which will surely send the boule awry.

Have you ever watched one of those movies where the souped-up hot car is accelerating away at full speed and the rear tires are going from side to side as the rear tires try to lay down all of the power?

That's not unlike we, as club players, as we try and accelerate our arm from a standing start to a full speed release of the boule. You don't believe me? I've spent many an hour as an umpire watching players do the exact thing I have described. Imagine, if you will, even a centimeters' wide variation in your forward accelerating arm and the effect it will have on your eventual release point and the resultant landing point. Generally, the side-to-side variation can be as great as an inch or two at the landing point with deeply disappointing results.

Generally, this will result in the throwing arm being slightly crooked. Perhaps it happens because the throwing arm is already tensed as you prepare to accelerate the arm. However it happens, the end result is usually a lack of accuracy in that the boule thrown will generally be a good one if it lands within a meter of the line of the jack.

If I may be so bold as to put forth yet another piece of advice, it would be this:

Swing your arm back and forth a couple of times to get what you feel is the appropriate forward motion and use *that momentum* to release your boule on its trajectory.

Think twice before you go for a long throw.

And while I am on the topic of your arm swing, this is also something to think about.

When we release the boule, I would generally suggest for the *average club player* that you try not to take your arm above the horizontal when you are in an upright position. As soon as your arm goes higher than the horizontal, your head also wants to move upward. Straight away, you are losing sight of your landing point. Remember in the 'New way of aiming' and the 'New way of Shooting', we have gone to a little effort to determine our landing point so it would seem a little inappropriate to lose that advantage.

Those players who use the Plombee technique usually end up with their head looking up to the sky. If you don't believe me, watch them! I have no idea what they would use as a reference mark for their landing point, but they still persist with that method, and it seems to work for those players. I have to say that they mostly tend to sacrifice a little accuracy for the ability to overcome an unforgiving terrain. I should add that I'm fine with that technique but it's not a technique that suits my style of play. Maybe it's because I don't claim to understand their tactics at this highest level. Maybe it's because they have seen the big-name players do it, and they feel........ Whatever. This book is for the average club player who has a desire to improve themselves.

For myself, when playing at my home terrain which has a fairly thick layer of small stones as its top surface, I find I often stretch my landing point out to perhaps 75% of the distance. I have found that with a deliberate effort, I can pick out my landing point and not raise my head as my arm goes above the horizontal. It does take an effort, but I find it worthwhile.

Setting yourself up in your stance and posture.

This is something of a follow on from the previous topic.

We have seen the top-level golfers etc who put their everything into their golf swing in an effort to get the ball to go a little further?

Given that the roots of petanque go back to finding an easier game for old Bocce (or Jeu Provencal) players to retire to, it seems a little odd that we have so many club players today who are willing to contort their bodies into all sorts of ungodly shapes to get a boule just ten meters away. By all means get comfortable with your posture but is there really a need to twist the body out of shape to get the boule just ten meters away?

I have just watched a game between two top French teams. The Shooter on team A adopted this position before his release of the shot. His torso was bent below the horizontal and his throwing arm was now beyond the vertical. Try to imagine the effort and strain that put him under. Once he unwound his body, he released the boule at a fair rate of knots and missed! It seemed to be quite an anticlimax. His opposition, by comparison, seemed to be more relaxed. He only curled his wrist into his forearm before releasing the shot. The bent-out-of-shape shooter was hitting at 50% and the more relaxed shooter was hitting at around 65%.

At our club, we have a number of players who are seventy plus years old and still enjoying their game. A number of them are still quite competitive. Yet they don't see the need to contort themselves unduly. An upright posture and an arm that doesn't go above the horizontal should well be within their capabilities to put a boule at or around the ten-meter mark. A flick of the wrist during release will also help the boule go a little further. It's not for me to say how individual players should hold themselves in the circle but I can't help but think they are not helping their game too much or just making the game too complicated.

Your back swing

Believe it or not, the back swing is important. earlier in the book I made a suggestion about not letting your throwing arm hang at your side and then accelerate into your throw from that position. A number of coaches will suggest that you take your throwing arm and lift it as high as you can in your backswing. I don't totally endorse that position if your target is only around six or seven meters away. The thing I do endorse is that you should get into to the habit of a backswing as it is one less thing to worry about in your forward swing, worrying about how much you need to 'hurl' the boule to get it to the nine-meter mark etc.

Your follow through

It's only a suggestion, but it works for me. Try to maintain the form (or shape) in your hand to beyond the release point and allow your hand to follow through up to a level approximately level with your shoulders. It's also fairly important that you try and keep your hand level in the follow through as it then gives your hand every chance to impart some backspin.

What about your spare arm?

It's not something that the books cover, but your non-throwing arm plays a vital role in helping you to maintain your balance. As a suggestion, your arm should probably move away from your body and the action of swinging your throwing arm will automatically put your non-throwing arm in the appropriate position to maintain your balance.

Standing in the circle

When you are in the circle, the world should stop for you for a short while. The players and spectators should shut up and not make any movements to distract you. You have a full minute to play your boule. It is entirely up to you how you choose to play that boule. You can stand behind the circle and pick your target line and your landing point.

When I say savor that moment, I am being serious!

An average end may take anything up to ten or 12 minutes. You may only have two boules to play but you are a vital part of your team so if you need to take your full minute, you should take it. Don't ever be nervous when you step into the circle. Savor the moment! You are going to have a go at being the vital cog in your team machine. Take your time to determine your line. Take your time to determine your landing point. Decide what type of shot you want to play, be it a point or a shoot. Relax and build up to the release of your boule.

If your boule becomes a counter or takes out the target boule, accept your teams' plaudits. If it doesn't hit the spot that you wanted it to go to, then relax and remember that you tried your very best. You may have another shot, or you may not. It does not matter. What does matter is that You gave it your best shot, so step out of the circle and then relax!

When you step out of the circle, RELAX!!

This takes me neatly onto my next point. When you step out of the circle, please make an effort to relax. Become almost a disinterested bystander. There is absolutely nothing you can do to help the next person in the circle. Whether that person is your teammate or your opponent the last thing you need to do is to be tense. For the minute someone else is in the circle your role is to be relaxed and levelheaded. When the next person has played their boule, then, and only then, bring your attention back to the game and perhaps you can offer advice to your teammate or congrats for a good shot played. Being tense and nervous will have no effect on the next shot, other than to make you feel very tired at the end of the game!

If a shot or point doesn't hit the spot, what then?

Whatever happens, step out of the circle. Walk up to the head and see if you can determine where your shot or point went awry. Did it deviate because you imparted some sidespin? That would be indicated by an ever-increasing curve on the path of your boule. Did it deviate because it hit a sharp stone in the depths of the divot you made? That would be indicated by a deflection on the boule that went straight in its new direction. Was your initial aim awry? It should only take a few seconds to check. Really, at this point you are, or should be, focusing on calming down and getting ready to play your next shot. The act of walking up to the head should just be a part of your switching off from a shot that went wrong. Please be aware that the previous shot of yours now does not really matter. Honestly, it does not really matter! It is now simply a piece of history! Walk back to the rear of the circle and realign with your target point and your landing point and step back into the circle and relax!

Great games for three players

Often you will find yourself with three players and, as we know, Petanque is a game for singles or doubles or triples.

There are two games that I find are both interesting and still demanding.

The first game is a game called "Shanghai" based on the British-invented darts games. Here is how to play the game:

Each player plays with three boules, and they play against the other two players. Once the Jack is thrown, the first player throws out a pointing shot. The next player can decide whether to shoot or point and then the third player also has the same choices. After each player has played one boule, the player with the boule farthest from the Jack plays the next boule. And the player farthest from the jack is the next player to play as the game progresses.

When the end is completed, the player closest to the Jack gets three points for that boule. The player with the second closest boule gets two points and the player with the third closest boule gets one point.

The score tallies up to 21 points and the first player to 21 wins the game. The refinement with this game is if a player gets all their three boules closest to the Jack, they get the six points, but they are also awarded the "Shanghai" and they win the game. The tactics become more involved when the other two players play as a team to stop the first player getting the 'Shanghai" and winning the game. Also, when the scores are getting towards the 21 points stage, often the other two players will combine their efforts to prevent the leading player going out.

The second game for three players is also a little tactical in its execution. Two players combine as a doubles team and the third player plays with six boules. So far so good. The tactical refinement is that the player playing with six boules has to nominate one of the two sets of three boules they are playing with as the set they will only shoot with!

That player is now only allowed to point with one set of boules and shoot with the other set of boules. The opponents are also obliged to have one player that points and one player that must shoot their three boules. The score goes up to 13 points as per the normal game. It's on the opposition team to call out if they believe the opponent did not make a genuine attempt at a shot with their nominated shooting set of boules. It's a very good tactical game with the individual player having to think ahead as to how many shooting or pointing boules they have yet to play and when to use them.

Another great game I picked up from a local trainer, Graeme Morrison, is called tic-tac-toe.

Start by marking out a 'tic-tac-toe' square on the terrain. Make each square perhaps a couple of feet square (600 mm) and set the circle perhaps six meters from the tic-tac- toe markings. Each person on the team has a go at landing a boule inside a square of the design. If you get a boule inside the square a team mate gets the next go. The object of the game is to get a diagonal or equivalent line going. If a player does not manage to get their Boule in a square, the opposing team has their chance to try. The opposition has to throw to either block your line or complete their own line when they get their go. The winner is the team that gets their tic-tac-toe line first. Then both teams set the circle back at the seven meter line and try again.

It becomes a very tactical game as you try and stop the opponents completing their line before you do.

Anatomy of a Triples team

This is a quandary I see quite often because many teams don't realise the need to allocate roles to the individual. In a triples team there are three roles the team is often divided into.

The Pointer - is the individual that predominantly points.

The Shooter - is the individual who shoots.

The third player is called "*The Milieu*". This is the player who hopefully can do both the pointing and the shooting.

Most players can do a little bit of pointing and shooting. So how do we decide who fills which role? At a club level is where the top shooters are most rare.

The *shooter* is the person who is the best *shooter in the team.*

The *Pointer* is the person who is the best *pointer in the team (of the remaining two players)*

The *Milieu* is the *third person* in the team. Often, the Milieu is also the captain and can both point and shoot.

Over the many years I have played in triples teams it is important to decide who fills which role. In the top French teams, there are often three very good shooters who also point very well. However, they still generally put themselves into one of the positions mentioned above. But we are not talking about the top teams here, we are talking about the average club players.

And be very aware, that over a weekend or a day of play the shooter or pointer may lose their edge because of fatigue or the fact that 'this terrain just doesn't suit them'. Always be prepared to switch over an individual's designated role as pointer or shooter or Milieu if they are not going well. That is why you are a team. When one is not firing well, give them a bit of a break and let the milieu step up etc. While having a team talk, pre-tourney, our captain made the very sensible suggestion that we should swop our positions *before* it became necessary. Essentially, he made it fine for us to admit we were not happy with our pointing or shooting and that it was ok for us to ask for a break for an end or two or ten.

One other thing in a triples team. There should always be a Captain of the team. The team should always discuss their next shoot or point and decide on which course of action to take, or which side of the head they would prefer to use. If opinion is divided let the captain make the decision, and go with that decision. If the decision was wrong, so be it, but at least some individual had the responsibility to make that decision.

Last but not least. We have all seen the club player that fancies themselves as the shooter. They will stand in the circle and fire a shoot down which misses. Before you can take stock of the situation, they have already fired another boule down (and probably missed again).

Always, always always, as the captain, stand near the head and be ready to walk onto the terrain with your hand up to stop the rapid-fire shooter in their tracks. If you have already wasted one boule with a miss, let's at least have a team talk to decide which way you wish to advance the game.

The best type of Opening point

There is no end of ways in which the opening point can go during an end. However, the flipside of that point is that it can sometimes determine the rest of the end for your team! If a pointer rolls a meter or so past the Jack, it almost seems to give confidence to the opposition who then roll a point to within an inch of the Jack. They have already noted your landing point which made your boule skip a meter past so they can easily make the adjustment to ensure their point is on the button.

For me the ideal pointing shot is perhaps six or so inches short of the Jack and right in line with the Jack.

It's a visual and mental block for the opponent who won't want to risk promoting your boule.

If they shoot it out it's already used up one of your opponent's boules. If they miss and have to take two shots at your boule, that's even better news.

If they try and go around our boule, generally speaking they will be at least eight inches away from the Jack so, again it will have used up two of our opponents' boules.

What will generally happen is that they will have a couple of goes at going around our boule before they actually have a go at shooting it. Now they have used up three of their boules.

Even if the opening boule is two feet short of the Jack, as long as it is reasonably in line with the Jack, it will cause the opponents some discomfort.

At a club level of play I find that the 'captain' will usually call for a pointer to enter the circle when there is a boule just in front of the Jack. Why? If you have a shooter available, send the shooter in! If the shooter misses with both boules, then it is already time to have the discussion on whether to close the head down. If the shooter hits, it may be time to let the other team try again. Either way, you are not in the position of having played four boules and then deciding to close the head down with just two boules remaining.

Shooting tips.

If the opponent's boule is at a level with the Jack and only an inch away, while it may look hard it has actually just become a whole lot easier. Instead of having a target a boule wide, your target has now become almost <u>two boules wide</u>, when you factor in the extra width of the Jack and extra latitude it gives to your next shot. If you take out the Jack with your shot it means you get a whole new end to set your advantage up with.

If you have a couple of opponents boules a foot in front of the Jack, they are not hindering you. They are providing a nice <u>wide</u> target for you to smash your next shot into.

If you have a couple of your own boules a foot in front of the Jack, that is not a hindrance. It's an excellent opportunity for you to use the 'point with attitude' style of shot and <u>promote your boules</u> forward.

If you have a couple of your opponent's boules six inches behind the Jack and holding, you are not disadvantaged as you have a <u>nice wide target</u> to rest your 'point with attitude' boule onto.

I guess the point I am making here is that you should always look on the positive side when it becomes your turn to play a boule.

Every game is a final

Even in the early rounds of pool play, the result is important. So, if you continue to play as a well organised and disciplined team, you will still be a formidable opponent. I have seen a few teams that lift themselves for the knockout stages and I can only wonder why they bother. Every game is important in a tournament and the opponents should be treated as worthy adversaries. By all means make it a friendly affair but that does not mean you should ease off if your opposition is a weak team. The other top teams will play the same opponents and beat them soundly, so don't feel too harsh when you beat a team 13-0 instead of waiting for them to get a couple of points to make them feel good!

Could you be an umpire?

A Player inadvertently throws a teammates boule. Does that boule count?

Chapter 9: The mind game.

When we first started playing petanque there were no end of teams that were better skilled than we were. That did not stop us from entering tournaments. Insofar as we were concerned, we were only going to get better by playing against better teams. It was something of a revelation for us that the top teams would often offer friendly advice. The 'wannabe's' always seemed to want to fanny us so they could get maximum points to proceed further. But the top teams in this sport were a delight to play against.

It became something of an issue to not get "Fannied"!

As we grew in the game, we became less worried about getting fannied, but we still realised that there were better teams out there.

It soon got to the stage where I'd look at the better team and think to myself "we're worth at least four points against these guys."

If we got more than four points, I'd count it as a mini or a moral win for us and the next time we met I would raise the bar and we would have to get six points. Don't get me wrong on this logic, there were always going to be better teams to meet on the piste. This was my personal way of setting a standard for us to improve to.

Nowadays, no team is unbeatable when we walk on the terrain! They can have a bad day and we can have a good day and the win goes in our column!

What I would like you to do as a team is use the head game to your advantage.

And there are so many ways to get on top of the head game!

- Don't start with a negative mindset. If you believe you are in for a hiding before you even step on the terrain, guess what, you are! Every team is beatable.
- They can have an off day and you can have a good day.
- If they have a good shooter, don't make it too easy for them. Put your boules up against their boules. (Remember the newtons cradle effect).
- If you can put your boule behind their boule, it's always harder to shoot your boule out if they have to come over the top or get past their own boule to take yours out.
- Remember the average club shooter will only hit one boule in two attempts. If you put a good holding boule in it should take at least two of their boules to take it out.
- Listen to what the opponents are saying. If they have a righthanded player who says they don't like to come in on the left-hand side, force them to play shots on the left-hand side.
- Watch for their landing point. If it rolls a meter past the Jack, you have a built-in ready reference (their divot) to make an adjustment with your pointer.
- If they only seem to have players that like to point straight, build a wall in front of the Jack that forces them to go wider.
- If they have a strong shooter, force that player to use up their boules early. Often, a team with a good shooter will fall apart when they no longer have a shooter to call on.
- Look at the shot or point you need to play next. Let the whole team make the decision as to whether it is a point or a shot or a 'point with attitude'.
- Always have a time in each end decided between your team where you decide to defend the end.
- Analyse your opposition. Do they have a good shooter? Do they have two? Is the terrain surface the type of surface that helps or hinders their pointer?

- Most teams, if they have not read this book, have a couple of pointers who try and roll the boule straight to the jack. If their boule rolls away to one side, they try and correct it by throwing another boule. If they had any tactical nous they would try and use the rolling away of their boule to get round any barrier in front. It happens so often it's fun to watch!

Last but not least, when you are in the pools section of play, always remember that any points you score can help you to progress to the next round, so never give up!

I have seen many of the very top teams have a bad day and lose 13-0. For many of the top teams, getting beaten by a team of no names is bad enough, but think what it does for you reputation when it gets known that you beat (insert whichever team you want) in a recent competition. In a recent tourney our team beat one of the favoured teams 13-2. It was a surprise to us, as well as we thought it would be much closer. Imagine how satisfying it was to hear the other teams saying '....... ....." just got beat 13-2. Unfortunately, no one seemed to realise it was our team that beat his team. It was still good to hear it, though!

I said earlier in the book about teams believing you are 'easy beats' and how it gives them the confidence to attack you with flair. If the word gets around that you beat a certain team convincingly, think how it makes them look at you with a newfound respect. Suddenly their shooting success ratio takes a downward dive.

Trust me on the above. It does happen! (And it is so good when it does happen).

Don't see any other boule except the one you are targeting.

This gets right into your mindset or headspace. When you are standing in the circle and looking down the terrain at the head, clear your head of everything but the target boule or the Jack. Yes, there might be one of your boules an inch or so to one side and if you move it, it could give the opponents three points. More importantly if you send your boule down and it does its job correctly, you might end up with four points.

I suppose it comes down to your own level of confidence. One thing I learned in my training days was to always focus on the target. You have a much greater chance of hitting your target if you don't focus on other potential problems.

Learn from your opponents.

What can you learn from your opponents? In a game I played last weekend where I was an invited player to a makeup team, I overheard an opposition player say to his teammate that he hated it when their captain put the Jack too close to the side string line. As a good team member, I had a quiet word to my team captain about that players comment. When it became our turn to place the Jack on the terrain, our captain placed the Jack within a couple of inches from the stringline. We scored five points! It seemed that none of their team liked the jack being near the string line. We repeated the process a couple of ends later and won the game 13-5. So, is it worthwhile listening to what your opponents say and their play?

Let's take a few examples:

Scenario one- when they push the Jack out to their preferred length, you should be aware of that and react accordingly. If they put the Jack to seven meters because their shooter is not strong at the longer lengths, it does give you an indication that you should be trying the Jack at a length of nine meters plus.

Scenario two- if they roll their boule five feet past the Jack, make a note of their landing point. It should be telling you to perhaps consider a landing point two or three feet closer to the circle.

Scenario three - if their boule hits a particularly thick (or thin) part of the terrain and comes to a sudden stop, it should make you aware of that particular issue and make you either pick a different line for your boule or perhaps to add a little more 'oomph' to your throw.

Could you be an umpire?

One of your opponents is wearing gloves. Is that allowed?

Chapter 10: Keep a count of the boules to play.

Keep a count of the boules to play and work out who holds the advantage!

Each team has six boules to play, so who holds the advantage?

Imagine this scenario, your team threw the first boule and the opposition effectively wasted all of their six boules by shooting etc. Obviously, you hold the advantage as you are holding the point and you still have five boules to play.

And now think of the opposite scenario. They hold five in hand, and they are holding the point.

At what point should you have decided to try and close the head down to make it difficult for them to score more than one point?

Another scenario.

You shoot your first boule and miss. You shoot a second boule and miss. Do you shoot a third boule?

If both teams have three boules left and you hold the point, I still believe you have the advantage because they have to try to make you play your boules before they play their last boule or two.

I think it is mainly in my role as an umpire that I get to watch the head games between the teams on the terrain. I'd have to say, it is fun to watch!

I'm surprised how many teams will shoot perhaps four boules and then have a team conference to discuss whether they should consider closing the head down. For myself, the correct time for this decision is after you have played two boules!

There are any number of variables to consider. Does your team have a good shooter? (So why did they miss the first two boules?) How strong is your pointer? Can they, with reasonable certainty, get a boule or two closer to the head?

How good is the opposition shooter? If the opposition is shooting 'everything', is it time to keep pointing into the head and crowd the head so they have difficulty getting a clear shot?

Remember the very best shooters will only hit 4 out of 5. The shooters you meet on an average competition will probably only hit one from two shots or one shot in three attempts.

I guess the point I am making here is to be aware of your opposition and how many boules you have and the opposition has.

I do watch the big boys play on You tube and it almost seems like a 'point and shoot game'. One team points the boule close to the jack and the other team sends in their shooter to shoot the first teams boule out. Until one of the opponents misses their shot and then the whole scene changes. Or perhaps the team that is shooting comes up with a 'Carreau' and the opposition now have to bring in their shooter. One thing I have noticed is that many of the teams that win a point and then start first on the next end seem to struggle to wrest the advantage from the opposition. It often works out that one team gets a point, then the opposition gets a point or two and the roles are reversed. There are a couple of players I admire that don't seem to fall into this trap. Christian Fazzino is one and Phillippe Quintais is another. Michael Bonnetto and Diego Rizzi also seem to want to be in control of the oppositions tactics and it often works for them also.

They seem to be always aware of the number of boules left to the opposition and plan accordingly.

If I may be so bold, let me put in the following for you to consider.

You pointed first and are holding the shot approx. six inches in front of the jack.

They have six boules; they shoot and miss.

They have five boules left, they shoot and miss again.

They have four boules left, they shoot again and hit your boule sending it over the dead boule line. Their boule is now a meter past the jack.

Your team points again. You have five boules left. You point to within a foot of the jack.

They point just inside your boule. You have four boules left and they have only three remaining. Do you shoot their holding boule?

Think about who has the advantage. For myself I'd consider that we have the advantage, and I would try and shoot their boule out. If I shoot their boule we are still holding and we have the advantage in that we have the same number of boules but are holding and forcing them to play their next boule which gives us the advantage again.

They decide to point, and we are still holding the point after they have played. They now have to play another of their two remaining boules. Advantage is now firmly in our court. How do we maximize that advantage?

There are so many variables at this stage of the game that it becomes almost impossible to cover them all.

The key thing for you, as captain, to think about is the question of who holds the advantage and how do you maximize the opportunity.

If the situation is reversed, is your best opportunity to close the head down and make it difficult for them to score any extra points? If your shooter is only an average player, quite often the best you can do is to close the head down. The brave captain will look to raise this question after two boules have been played. The other type of captain may decide to hope for a bit of luck and not make the decision until four of their boules have been played.

So which type of captain are you?

Umpire question.

Does an umpire have to first give a yellow card as a warning for bad behaviour, or can they go straight to a red card if the offence is sufficient to merit that punishment?

Chapter 11: Practice routines

A good friend of ours and I used to travel to tourneys together. We would always try and get to the tourney terrain the day before and practice our shooting, which was what we were both lesser skilled at. We would send a boule down to six meters and then try and shoot it. If the boule was hit, we would move forward until the target was again around six meters away. We would keep count up to ten and then start again. Best of two out of three and the winner had a beer at the other's expense.

The reason I put that one in is that it is always a great idea to have a goal or specific idea in mind when you set out for a practice session. Below I'll set up a few practice sessions for you to consider.

Practice makes perfect.

I am sure you have heard the legend that Dylan Rocher shoots 1000 boules a day to keep his eye in. The same legend would have it that it was Marco Foyot or Phillipe Quintais etc. To be honest, I have seen the way these players shoot, and I am fairly positive their arms would be dropping off if they were to attempt to put in in even one tenth of that effort. All of the above guys are also very good pointers, often using the three-quarter lob or Plombee to point. I really don't think they do that much practice!!

Notwithstanding that point, I am going to recommend you commit to some regular practice routines. I am making the strong suggestion that you radically change your game to accommodate the new techniques I am suggesting. If the old techniques you used were working for you, why did you buy this book?

Routines are a form of habit. Habit is what we pick up by practicing these routines. I think you would benefit from these new habits so I'm suggesting you commit to the following routines to replace the bad habits you have picked up.

Probably out of all of the practice routines I'd suggest your first sessions should be reminding yourself how easy it is to throw a straight point and then committing to always picking out a landing point (on your target line). But that is over to you, so I have set down the following for you to think about. I'd always suggest you team up with a partner to do your practice sessions. When you have thrown six boules, it becomes their turn to throw, while you take a break, and your turn to give constructive pointers to your mate.

Practice 1. a straight-line pointing throw.

Of all the things we do in this game this is the one we do most often so it should be the one we are most consistent with.

The simplest way to practice this point is to throw your boule along the string lines between each terrain! Firstly, it checks out how well you are hitting your landing point (the String line) and secondly, by checking the rollout, it is a clear indicator of how straight your pointing is going. Start at six meters and then move to seven meters and increase accordingly. If you do get a rollout to either side, check the divot you made for any stones that may have made your boule kick away.

Having a mate practice along with you gives the following advantage. Get your mate to stand at the opposite end of the terrain. When your boule leaves your hand, your mate should be able to quickly mimic your final hand position. So, if your boule goes to the left, and your mates hand is indicating in that direction, you can be pretty much aware that you put a spin on the boule!

Remember, for the straight point you need to remember the following.

Keep your fingers straight.

Keep your fingers held together.

Get your hips out of the way.

Practice 2-Aiming in a new way!

Set up 2 boules at the six-meter mark around two feet apart, and one boule approximately midway between the two and perhaps a foot or so beyond.

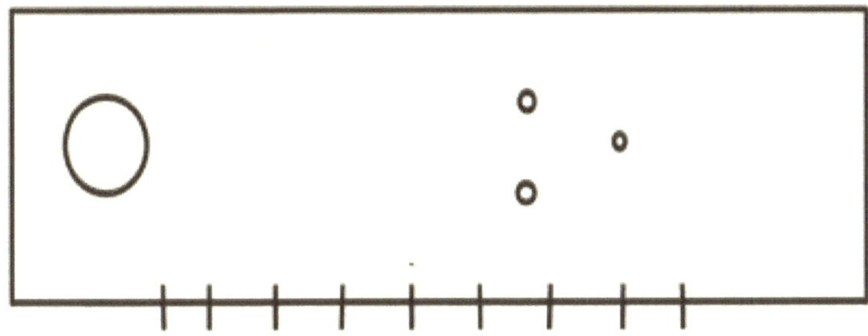

Diagram 11.1 Practice the 'aiming in a new way' technique.

Stand behind the circle to select your landing point, and then step in the circle and aim for the boule in the middle with a straight point. Remember, you are only going to point your boule to the target boule so you only need to work out your landing point. Try it for three goes. If you are happy with the result, move the front row of boules to around 15 inches apart and try again. When you are happy with that, move the front row of boules to twelve inches apart and try again. When you get confident you should be able to have the front row of boules no more than six inches apart and still be confidently capable of hitting or resting on the target boule. Always remember that if you are pointing in a straight line, the problem that makes you nervous about pointing between a six inch gap, is entirely inside your head!

I suppose the main difficulty with this new method of pointing is hitting your landing point every time. If that is a problem for you, try this. Mark your landing point only a couple of meters from the circle and try again. Then increase your landing point to perhaps 2.5 meters and try again. When you are confident at 2.5 meters, mark your landing point at 3 meters and so on. It's like any other new technique you try, it will take time and practice. But if you genuinely wish to improve your standard of play, this is definitely the way to start your advancement.

Practice 3. Pick your landing point.

Once you have the straight point to a level you are happy with, for me, the next most important thing is being able to pick out your landing point and hit it every time (or get really close to it).

You and your partner in practice should pace out the terrain and mark the terrain at three, four, five, six, seven, eight, nine and ten meter mark.

This is a practice for both of you to participate in. You are first. Point a boule to the six-meter mark by getting your landing point at the three-meter mark. Next boule, try the four-meter mark and finally your last boule is targeting the five-meter mark. Give yourself points under the Shanghai system. Now try the seven-meter mark for your distance. A halfway lob should land around three and a half meters. The three-quarter lob should see you pick a landing point around the five meter mark. A Plombee' shot should see your landing point on the six meter mark.

Keep going until you are getting out to the ten meter mark for your target jack. If you are struggling on any distance, that is the one you probably need to practice more.

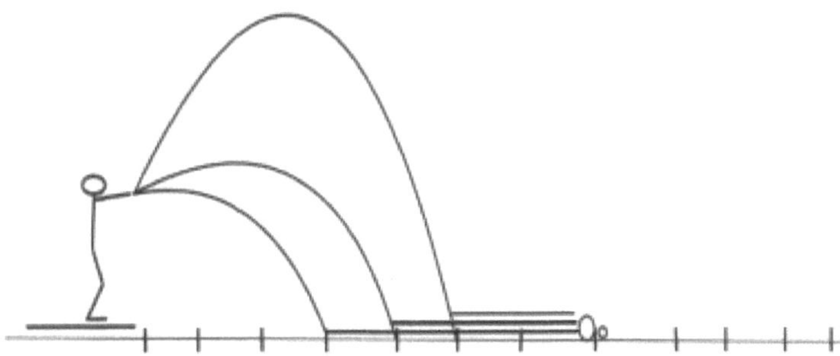

Diagram 11.2 Practice hitting the landing point.

Practice 4. Pointing with attitude

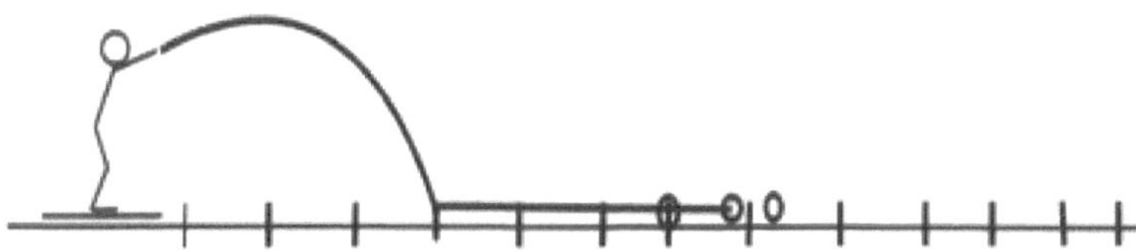

Diagram 11.3. Practice your 'Pointing with Attitude.'

Again, this is an exercise to practice with a friend. Practicing this technique is not too complicated. Put a boule on the terrain at six meters and another boule at seven meters. Point your boule so that it goes past the six-meter mark but not past the seven-meter mark. You are not trying to hit the boules at this point. You are only using the boules on the terrain as a distance marker. When you are happy you have this down, put the boule at six meters out to the eight-meter mark. Now you point the boule, so it goes past the seven-meter mark but not the eight-meter mark. Carry on doing this exercise to the nine- and ten-meter mark until you feel confident you have the control in your pointing. Now repeat the exercise by placing the boule at the six-meter mark in the centre of the terrain. Point (with attitude) to not beyond the seven-meter mark and try to take out, or nudge, the boule at six meters. If you are pointing in a straight line, it should not be a major obstacle to hit the six-meter boule. This technique, of course, is to be used in conjunction the 'New way of Aiming' technique if you want your game to raise itself to the next level. Remember, you are aiming to take the boule out at the first mark and stop before the second mark!

<u>Practice 5. Spinning the boule from the left to right with side spin.</u>

Now spend a little time aiming the boule a couple of feet to the left (or right) and practice making that shot work for you. Try it first by placing a spare boule at six meters and aiming your boule a couple of feet to the left. When you can get comfortable with the results of that shot, move the target boule out to seven meters and practice again. Obviously the boule will travel as far as the momentum you put on it, so you will have to adjust the amount of travel you put on the boule.

From a personal point of view, I found that my spinning shot from left to right worked better for me than the other way. So, I practiced just that shot and it got me out of trouble on quite a few occasions. It got to the stage where I had to make a conscious decision before I played the boule as to whether I wanted the boule go straight or come in from left to right. And of course, as I got further into a weekend of tournament play occasionally I put totally the wrong spin on a boule and the boule started two feet to the left and ended a further two feet to the left as I had put the spin for a straight shot on a boule I had aimed to the left. It happens!

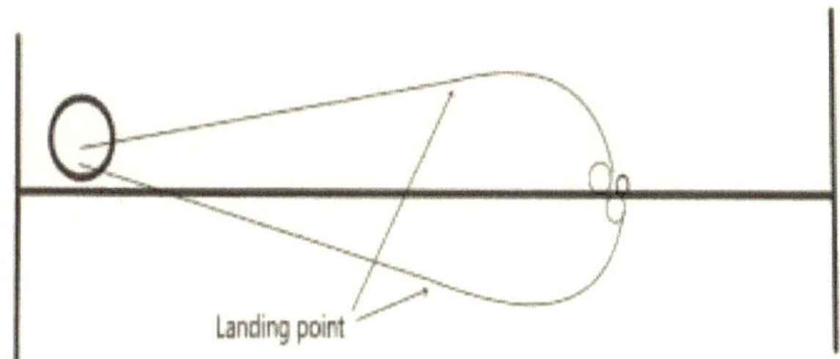

Diagram 11.4. Practice the 'spinning from the side' shots.

Practice 6. Your Plombee shot.

Practicing this style is not so difficult. Place a broom or rake on the ground at five or six meters from the circle. Lob the boule with sufficient height that it lands just beyond the marker and has a rollout that is less than a meter long. The length of rollout is the most important factor here and this length of lob is usually used for the most unforgiving terrains. If you are getting too much rollout, try lobbing the boule to a greater height. When you are getting a reasonable amount of success with the marker at the shorter distance, place the marker perhaps another meter away from the circle and try again.

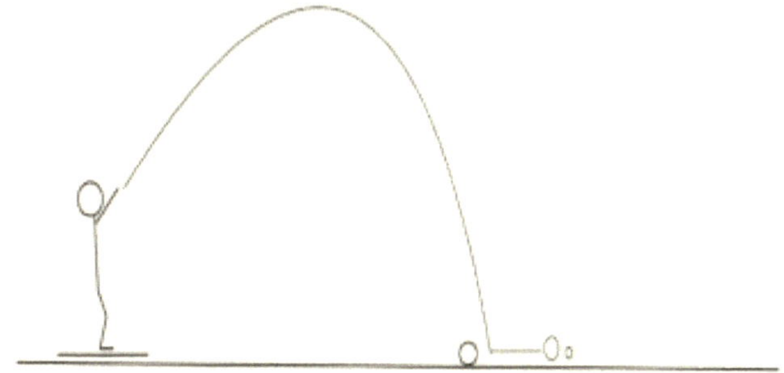

Diagram 11.5. Practice your 'Plombee' shots

<u>Practice routine 7. Land in an existing divot!</u>

An excellent practice routine is to try to land your boule in a divot hole.

Because the divot is usually only a couple of inches wide, and four inches long, it becomes a real test of your accuracy at picking your landing point. Start with a boule at perhaps three meters and then increase as your confidence grows.

<u>A couple of Gary Player stories to illustrate my point</u>:

In the Practice round of one of the larger tourneys on the USA golf circuit, Gary Player landed a ball in the left-hand bunker adjacent to the green. The ball rolled on over the bunker and ended up around four feet from the pin. The guy he was playing with chivvied Gary about being such a lucky player. Gary immediately dropped another ball on the tee and repeated the exact same shot with the nearly identical result. Then Gary turned to his playing buddy and said, "It's amazing, the more I practice, the luckier I get!"

Second Gary Player story:

During the same round, Gary put one down the fairway with a gentle left to right swing and landed in the middle of the fairway. His buddy put nearly the same shot down and it just caught the edge of the rough, bounced badly and landed deep in the rough. While chivvying Gary, he also was having a go at himself. "We both put the ball over the left-hand bunker. Yours landed in the middle of the fairway and mine landed in the rough."

Gary never looked at his buddy, he just continued walking to his ball. Then he said, "The difference between us is that you put your ball over the left-hand bunker. If you look at that bunker, there is a rake in it with a tooth missing. I aimed to put my ball right over the top of that missing tooth on the rake. But it could just be that I'm so lucky."

Could you be an umpire?

This happened to me when I was an umpire. The Jack was travelling along the string having been hit by a boule. One team were convinced it had gone over the line and the other team were equally convinced it had not gone over.

Chapter 12:
The Rules of the game and a few comments

This set of rules were taken from the web. I have spent many an hour in research and also with the Umpires set of research tools. What I have set out below may well be my personal opinions and comments, but they are well researched. I am also aware that these interpretations may vary from one country to another as the use in the translated version may place a particular emphasis on one meaning of the word which may differ in another English-speaking country. If you have any queries, please consult a local national umpire who will be happy to give their thoughts on a rule interpretation.

Petanque rules 2021 FIPJP (UK English)

OFFICIAL RULES FOR THE SPORT OF PÉTANQUE

Applicable to all territories of the national federations, members of the FIPJP

Note: These rules were reviewed and amended by Mike Pegg and Claude Azema in 2021. It should also be emphasised these rules were amended and accepted by the FFPJP in December 2020. The original rules were executed in the French Language. It is quite within reason to assume that in the translation to English by Mike and Claude there may be some minor alterations that would not readily translate from the original French Version. To that end, there will always be some minor variations on a regional basis. Many individual federations may have a separate 'Code of conduct' to cover these minor variations. It is always an option to consider the 'Spirit of the law' in preference to the 'letter of the law'.

GENERAL RULES[1]

Article 1, Composition of teams.[2]

Article 2, Characteristics of approved boules.[3]

Article 2a, Penalties for irregular boules.[4]

Article 3, Approved jacks.[5]

Article 4, Licences.[6]

PLAY[7]

Article 5, Area of play and terrain rules.[8]

Article 6, Start of play and rules regarding the circle.[9]

Article 7, Valid distances for the thrown jack.[10]

Article 8, For the thrown jack to be valid.[11]

---

1. *https://petanquerules.wordpress.com/petanque-rules-2020-fipjp-uk-html/#_Toc60220685*

2. https://petanquerules.wordpress.com/petanque-rules-2020-fipjp-uk-html/#_Toc60220686

3. https://petanquerules.wordpress.com/petanque-rules-2020-fipjp-uk-html/#_Toc60220687

4. https://petanquerules.wordpress.com/petanque-rules-2020-fipjp-uk-html/#_Toc60220688

5. https://petanquerules.wordpress.com/petanque-rules-2020-fipjp-uk-html/#_Toc60220689

6. https://petanquerules.wordpress.com/petanque-rules-2020-fipjp-uk-html/#_Toc60220690

7. *https://petanquerules.wordpress.com/petanque-rules-2020-fipjp-uk-html/#_Toc60220691*

8. https://petanquerules.wordpress.com/petanque-rules-2020-fipjp-uk-html/#_Toc60220692

9. https://petanquerules.wordpress.com/petanque-rules-2020-fipjp-uk-html/#_Toc60220693

10. https://petanquerules.wordpress.com/petanque-rules-2020-fipjp-uk-html/#_Toc60220694

Article 9, Dead Jack during an end.[12]

Article 10, Displacement of obstacles.[13]

Article 11, Changing of jack or boule.[14]

JACK[15]

Article 12, Jack masked or displaced.[16]

Article 13, Jack moved into another game.[17]

Article 14, Rules to apply if the jack is dead.[18]

Article 15, Positioning the jack after it has been stopped.[19]

BOULES[20]

Article 16, Throwing of the first and following boules.[21]

Article 17, Behaviour of players and spectators during a game.[22]

Article 18, Throwing of the boules and boules going outside the terrain.[23]

---

11. https://petanquerules.wordpress.com/petanque-rules-2020-fipjp-uk-html/#_Toc60220695

12. https://petanquerules.wordpress.com/petanque-rules-2020-fipjp-uk-html/#_Toc60220696

13. https://petanquerules.wordpress.com/petanque-rules-2020-fipjp-uk-html/#_Toc60220697

14. https://petanquerules.wordpress.com/petanque-rules-2020-fipjp-uk-html/#_Toc60220698

15. *https://petanquerules.wordpress.com/petanque-rules-2020-fipjp-uk-html/#_Toc60220699*

16. https://petanquerules.wordpress.com/petanque-rules-2020-fipjp-uk-html/#_Toc60220700

17. https://petanquerules.wordpress.com/petanque-rules-2020-fipjp-uk-html/#_Toc60220701

18. https://petanquerules.wordpress.com/petanque-rules-2020-fipjp-uk-html/#_Toc60220702

19. https://petanquerules.wordpress.com/petanque-rules-2020-fipjp-uk-html/#_Toc60220703

20. *https://petanquerules.wordpress.com/petanque-rules-2020-fipjp-uk-html/#_Toc60220704*

21. https://petanquerules.wordpress.com/petanque-rules-2020-fipjp-uk-html/#_Toc60220705

22. https://petanquerules.wordpress.com/petanque-rules-2020-fipjp-uk-html/#_Toc60220706

Article 19, Dead boules.[24]

Article 20, Stopped boules.[25]

Article 21, Time allowed to play.[26]

Article 22, Displaced boules.[27]

Article 23, A player throwing a boule other than his own.[28]

Article 24, Boules thrown contrary to the rules.[29]

POINTS AND MEASURING[30]

Article 25, Temporary removal of boules.[31]

Article 26, Measuring of points.[32]

Article 27, Removed Boules.[33]

Article 28, Displacement of the boules or the jack.[34]

Article 29, Boules equidistant from the jack.[35]

---

23. https://petanquerules.wordpress.com/petanque-rules-2020-fipjp-uk-html/#_Toc60220707

24. https://petanquerules.wordpress.com/petanque-rules-2020-fipjp-uk-html/#_Toc60220708

25. https://petanquerules.wordpress.com/petanque-rules-2020-fipjp-uk-html/#_Toc60220709

26. https://petanquerules.wordpress.com/petanque-rules-2020-fipjp-uk-html/#_Toc60220710

27. https://petanquerules.wordpress.com/petanque-rules-2020-fipjp-uk-html/#_Toc60220711

28. https://petanquerules.wordpress.com/petanque-rules-2020-fipjp-uk-html/#_Toc60220712

29. https://petanquerules.wordpress.com/petanque-rules-2020-fipjp-uk-html/#_Toc60220713

30. https://petanquerules.wordpress.com/petanque-rules-2020-fipjp-uk-html/#_Toc60220714

31. https://petanquerules.wordpress.com/petanque-rules-2020-fipjp-uk-html/#_Toc60220715

32. https://petanquerules.wordpress.com/petanque-rules-2020-fipjp-uk-html/#_Toc60220716

33. https://petanquerules.wordpress.com/petanque-rules-2020-fipjp-uk-html/#_Toc60220717

34. https://petanquerules.wordpress.com/petanque-rules-2020-fipjp-uk-html/#_Toc60220718

35. https://petanquerules.wordpress.com/petanque-rules-2020-fipjp-uk-html/#_Toc60220719

Article 30, Foreign bodies adhering to the boules or jack.[36]

Article 31, Complaints.[37]

DISCIPLINE[38]

Article 32, Penalties for absent teams or players.[39]

Article 33, Late arrival of players.[40]

Article 34, Replacement of a player[41]

Article 35, Penalties.[42]

Article 36, Bad weather[43]

Article 37, New phase of play.[44]

Article 38, Lack of Sportsmanship.[45]

Article 39, Bad behaviour[46]

Article 40, Duties of the Umpires.[47]

Article 41, Composition and decisions of the Jury.[48]

---

36. https://petanquerules.wordpress.com/petanque-rules-2020-fipjp-uk-html/#_Toc60220720

37. https://petanquerules.wordpress.com/petanque-rules-2020-fipjp-uk-html/#_Toc60220721

38. *https://petanquerules.wordpress.com/petanque-rules-2020-fipjp-uk-html/#_Toc60220722*

39. https://petanquerules.wordpress.com/petanque-rules-2020-fipjp-uk-html/#_Toc60220723

40. https://petanquerules.wordpress.com/petanque-rules-2020-fipjp-uk-html/#_Toc60220724

41. https://petanquerules.wordpress.com/petanque-rules-2020-fipjp-uk-html/#_Toc60220725

42. https://petanquerules.wordpress.com/petanque-rules-2020-fipjp-uk-html/#_Toc60220726

43. https://petanquerules.wordpress.com/petanque-rules-2020-fipjp-uk-html/#_Toc60220727

44. https://petanquerules.wordpress.com/petanque-rules-2020-fipjp-uk-html/#_Toc60220728

45. https://petanquerules.wordpress.com/petanque-rules-2020-fipjp-uk-html/#_Toc60220729

46. https://petanquerules.wordpress.com/petanque-rules-2020-fipjp-uk-html/#_Toc60220730

47. https://petanquerules.wordpress.com/petanque-rules-2020-fipjp-uk-html/#_Toc60220731

GENERAL RULES

Article 1, Composition of teams

Pétanque is a sport in which:

– 3 players play against 3 players (triples).

It can also be played by:

– 2 players against 2 players (doubles).

– 1 player against 1 player (singles).

In triples, each player uses 2 boules.

In doubles and singles, each player uses 3 boules.

No other formula is allowed.

(In the USA they also have another game played by four players using two Boules each. It's not an official game as per the FFPJP)

Article 2, Characteristics of approved boules

Pétanque is played with boules approved by the F.I.P.J.P. and which conform to the following criteria:

1) To be made of metal.

2) To have a diameter between 7.05 cm (minimum) and 8 cm (maximum).

3) To have a weight of between 650 grams (minimum) and 800 grams (maximum).

---

48. https://petanquerules.wordpress.com/petanque-rules-2020-fipjp-uk-html/#_Toc60220732

For competitions reserved for players who are aged 11 years or less in the year, they may use boules that weigh 600 grammes and are 65 mm in diameter provided that they are made under one of the approved labels.

The trademark of the manufacturer and the weight must be engraved on the boules and must always be legible.

The player's first and last names (or initials) may also be engraved on them, as well as various logos, initials, acronyms or similar detail, in accordance with the specifications relating to the manufacture of the boules. This would generally mean that the extra engraving can only be carried out by the manufacturer.

4) The boule must be hollow and not contain any material such as lead, sand, mercury etc. As a general rule, the boules must not be tampered with in any way, nor altered or modified after machining by the approved manufacturer. Importantly, re-tempering of the boules in order to modify the hardness applied by the manufacturer is forbidden.

Article 2a. Penalties for irregular boules

Any player guilty of breaking the above condition is immediately disqualified from the competition together with their partners.

If a boule not "tampered with" but worn, or of defective manufacture, does not pass the official examination successfully, or does not comply with the norms set out in paragraphs 1), 2) and 3) above, the player must change it. They may also change the set.

Complaints relating to these three paragraphs and made by players are admissible only before the start of a game. It is in the interests of the players, therefore, to ensure that their boules and those of their opponents comply with the above rules.

Complaints relating to 4) are admissible at any time during the game, but they must be made between ends. However, from the third end onwards, if a complaint made about the boules of an opponent is proved to be unfounded, 3 points will be added to the score of the opponent.

An umpire or the jury may, at any time, require examination of the boules of one or several players.

(In over 20 years of playing, I have only ever been asked once to present my boules to an official for examination. This was at a regional level competition, and we were asked by the umpires to swop our boules with our opponents for the opponents to examine the validity of the boules. Not the big frightener we were initially led to believe.)

Article 3, Approved jacks

Jacks are made of wood, or of a synthetic material bearing the manufacturer's mark and having obtained the FIPJP's approval in line with the precise specification relating to the required standards.

Their diameter must be 30 mm (tolerance: + or −1 mm). Their weight must be between 10 and 18 grams.

Painted jacks are authorised, but at no time must they, nor the jacks made of wood, be capable of being picked up with a magnet.

There are only two synthetic jacks approved by F.I.P.J.P. - OBUT and VMS. The approved synthetic jack must have the name of the manufacturer on it. Any synthetic jack without one of these brands written on it in relief and readable is not allowed in official competition.

Article 4, Licences

To be registered in a competition each player must present their licence, or, in accordance with the rules of their federation, a document proving their identity, and that they are a member of that federation.

This Article generally applies to international competitions only. Licences do not need to be produced by

PNZ affiliated players before domestic competitions in New Zealand. International players playing in a

restricted open (affiliated players only) competition while in New Zealand need to present a player licence.

before being eligible to play.

(Some countries do not actually issue a licence to players although they usually come up with something acceptable when the need arises for international competition. New Zealand is one of those countries).

PLAY

Article 5, Area of play and terrain rules

Pétanque is played on any surface. However, by the decision of the organising committee or an umpire, the teams may be required to play on a marked and defined terrain. In this case, the terrain for National Championships and International Competitions, must have the following minimum dimensions: 15 metres long x 4 metres wide.

For other competitions, the Federations may permit variations relative to these minimum dimensions, subject to them not being below 12 metres x 3 metres.

A playing area comprises of an indeterminate number of lanes defined by strings, the size of which must not interfere with the course of play.

These strings marking separate lanes are not dead ball lines except for those marking the end of the lane and the exterior of the terrain.

When the lanes are placed end to end, the end lines connecting the lanes are dead ball lines.

When the terrains of play are enclosed by barriers, these must be a minimum distance of 1 metre from the exterior line of the playing area.

Games are played to 13 points, with the possibility of leagues and qualifying heats being played to 11 points.

Some competitions can be organised within time limits. These must always be played within marked lanes and all the lines marking these lanes are dead ball lines.

(Across the world there are many differing or preferred surfaces for terrains. Most of them are quite forgiving but do beware of the couple that approach you, innocently, when they have seen you practising and suggest a little side bet would make it more interesting! I have been involved in a few countries where gambling on the result of a game is rife. And it usually involves a few hundred of the local currency.)

<u>Article 6, Start of play and rules regarding the circle</u>

The players must draw lots (toss a coin) to decide which team will choose the terrain, if it has not been allocated by the organisers, and to be the first to throw the jack.

(In answer to the inevitable query, the team that wins the toss (or drawing of lots) must play first, as in throw the jack out)

If the lane has been designated by the organisers, the jack must be thrown on this lane. The teams concerned must not go to a different lane without the umpire's permission.

(This rule also covers the question of a jack when first thrown on a designated lane going over the side string lines. The jack must be picked up and given to the opposing team to place on the terrain)

Any member of the team winning the draw chooses the starting point and places or traces a circle on the ground of a size that the feet of each player can fit entirely inside it. However, a drawn circle may not measure less than 35 cm or more than 50 cm in diameter.

Where a prefabricated circle is used, it must be rigid and have an internal diameter of 50 cm (tolerance: + or − 2 mm).

Folding circles are permitted but on condition they are of a model approved by the FIPJP with regard, in particular, to the rigidity.

The players are required to use the regulation circles provided by the organisers.

They must also accept the regulation rigid circles or the FIPJP approved folding circles provided by their opponent. If both teams have one of these circles, the choice will be decided by the team that won the draw.

The circle must be drawn (or placed) more than one metre from any obstacle and at least 1.5 metres from another throwing circle or jack in use.

The interior of the circle can be completely cleared of grit/pebbles etc. during the end but must be put back in good order when the end is over.

The players' feet must be entirely on the inside of the circle and not encroach on its perimeter and they must not leave it or be lifted completely off the ground until the thrown boule has touched the ground.

(Something to be aware of. When crouching in the circle to play a boule/ jack, the players heel can encroach over the inside edge of the circle, provided it does not touch the circle. If the player stands up and onto the circle before the boule/jack has touched the ground, they have stood on the perimeter of the circle, and not had both feet entirely inside the circle as required. A warning (yellow card) will be given.)

(A warning will also be given for the player who lifts a foot before the boule has touched the ground. It may take an eagle-eyed umpire to police this issue, but it does happen!)

No part of the body may touch the ground outside the circle. Any player not respecting this rule shall incur the penalties as provided in article 35.

(This may require a little expansion. It is acceptable for the player to touch the ground outside the circle when he is preparing to take his shot. This may be a reflection on the rule 10 where the player is allowed to tap the ground three times. However, once the player has 'launched' their boule into the air, they cannot touch the ground outside the circle until their boule has landed.)

As an exception, those disabled in the lower limbs are permitted to place only one foot inside the circle, but the other foot must not be in front of it. For players throwing from a wheelchair, at least one wheel (that on the side of the throwing arm) must rest inside the circle.

If a player picks up the circle when there are boules still to be played, the circle is replaced but only the opponents are allowed to play their boules.

(The circle is replaced by agreement of both teams. If the teams cannot agree, the umpire is called in to place the circle where it is 'obvious' the circle had originally been placed. If there is no obvious solution for the

umpire, the non-offending team should then have the right to place the circle where they believe it was originally.)

The circle is not considered to be an out of bounds area.

In all cases the circles must be marked before the jack is thrown.

The team that is going to throw the jack must erase all throwing circles near the one it is going to use.

The team winning the toss, or the previous end will have only one attempt to throw the jack. If this jack is not valid it is handed to the opponent who must place it on the terrain at a valid position. If the jack is not placed in a valid position by the second team, the player who placed it shall be subject to the penalties outlined in article 35, In the event of a repeat offence, a new card will be issued to the whole team, in addition to any cards previously received.

(An interesting discussion arose on the terrain this last weekend. The debate was whether the player who was 'placing' the jack had to literally bend down and touch the jack onto the ground, or whether it was ok to drop the jack onto the ground from a height of (say) a foot. There was a prominent NZ Umpire who insisted the jack had to be 'placed' on the ground, but I don't think I have ever seen anyone penalised for dropping the jack from above the ground. If this is a rule it is honoured in its absence by the top French teams! Andre Deramond (a Senior international umpire) has come out and stated that the Jack must be placed on the ground and not dropped from a height. Here in New Zealand, we take Andre's rulings as the law.)

The throwing of the jack by one member of the team does not imply that they are obliged to be the first to play.

It is the responsibility of the player who throws the jack to mark the circle. If the playing team does not mark the circle (properly), the opposing team may do so, and/or call the umpire. If a prefabricated circle is moved accidentally by a player and the circle was unmarked, it is to be replaced by agreement between the two teams as close as possible to where it was originally. If no agreement can be reached, the Umpire will place the circle in the most logical place. Failure to mark the circle correctly will warrant a warning (yellow card).

The players must mark the position of the jack initially and after each time it is moved. No claims will be allowed for an unmarked jack and the umpire will rule only on the position of the jack on the terrain.

(Previous markings should be erased each time a new position is marked. The marking of the jack can be carried out by either team, i.e., the opponents have the right to request that the playing team marks the jack, and to step onto the terrain to do so if the playing team does not. It should be noted that the last player whose boule caused the jack to be moved will, generally, be the player that is given the warning for not marking the position of the jack.)

Article 7. Valid distances for the thrown jack

For the thrown jack to be valid, the following conditions apply:

1) That the distance separating it from the internal edge of the circle must be

– 6 metres minimum and 10 metres maximum for Juniors and Seniors.

– For competitions intended for younger players, shorter distances may be applied.

*(When measuring for a valid jack, the end of the tape is placed on the **inside** edge of the circle, and the measurement is made to the closest edge of the jack.*

• If the closest edge of the jack is straddling the six-metre measure line it is not a valid throw. The complete jack must be over the 6m measurement.

• For a 10m measure, the closest edge of the jack must be inside or on the 10m line to be valid. Over the line is invalid.

2) That the throwing circle must be a minimum of 1 metre from any obstacle and 1.5 metres from another circle or jack in use.

3) That the jack must be a minimum of 50 cm from any obstacle and from the end line of the lane, it must also be a minimum of 1.5 metres from another jack or circle in use. *(note: no minimum distance is required from the "side" line that separates the lanes or the dead ball lines at the side of the lanes).*

(A common misconception is that the circle needs to be 50cm from the dead boule line at the 'circle' end of the terrain. It's a misconception!)

4) That the jack must be visible to the player whose feet are placed astride the extreme limits of the interior of the circle and whose body is absolutely upright. In case of dispute on this point, the umpire decides, without appeal, if the jack is visible.

At the following end the jack is thrown from a circle placed or traced around the point where it finished at the previous end, except in the following cases:

– The circle would be less than 1 metre from an obstacle, 1.5 metres from another circle or jack in use.

– The throwing of the jack could not be made to all regulation distances.

In the first case the player places or traces the circle at the regulation distance from the obstacle or object in question.

In the second case, the player may step back, in line with the previous end's play, without exceeding the maximum distance authorised for the throwing of the jack. This opportunity is offered only if the jack cannot be thrown to the maximum distance in any other direction.

If the circle is moved over the maximum authorised distance of 10.5m (10 + 0.5) by team A, two situations arise:

<u>Before</u> the jack is thrown: - The circle must be replaced to its original position or approximate position and team A retain the jack and proceed with the throw from the original position provided it is a valid distance of 6.5 m (6 + 0.5) from the dead boule line.

<u>After</u> the jack has been thrown by team A: - The circle must be replaced to its original position or approximate position and team B can move the circle in accordance with the rules to a valid distance and then place the jack.

If the jack has not been thrown in accordance with the rules defined above, the opposing team will place the jack in a valid position on the terrain. They may also move the circle back, in accordance with the conditions defined in these rules, if the first team's positioning of the circle did not allow the jack to be thrown the maximum distance.

(The circle must be moved and marked before placing the jack).

In any case, the team which lost the jack after the invalid throw must play the first boule.

The team that won the right to throw the jack have a maximum of one minute to do so. The team that won the right to place the jack after the unsuccessful throw of the opponent must do so immediately.

(If the jack is not placed in a valid position by team B:

◇ *Team B player receives a warning (yellow card);*

◈ Team B still has the right to re-place the jack in a valid position.)

Article 8, For the thrown jack to be valid.

If the thrown jack is stopped by an umpire, an opponent, a spectator, an animal, or any moving object, it is not valid and must be thrown again.

If the thrown jack is stopped by a member of the team the opponent will place the jack in a valid position.

If after the throwing of the jack, a first boule is played, the opponent still has the right to contest the validity of its position except in the case when the jack has been placed by a team member.

(That means the claimant cannot be on the side of the team member who placed the jack.)

Before the jack is given to the opponent to place, both teams must have recognised that the throw was not valid, or an umpire must have decided it to be so.

(The only valid way to decide this is by using a tape measure! If it is a close decision always use a tape!)

If the opponent has also played a boule, the jack is definitely deemed valid, and no objection is admissible.

(After the throw of the jack, one player from the team who won the previous end, or the toss, may, after marking the jack, step out the distance to estimate if the jack has been thrown to a valid distance. However, the opposition should not also walk the distance to confirm, as this is wasting the time of the player to play their first boule and they have no right to be on the terrain at this point. The opposing team may however immediately contest the validity of the jack and request that it be measured.)

(There is something of a misconception here. To say the opposing team "has no right to be on the terrain" is at best an over simplification of the rule. There are circumstances where the opposing team can step on the terrain, for instance when the first team is measuring a point.)

Article 9. Dead Jack during an end

The jack is dead in the following 7 cases:

1) When the jack is displaced into an out of bounds area, even if it comes back on to the authorised playing area. A jack straddling the boundary of an authorised terrain is valid. It becomes dead only after having completely crossed the boundary of the authorised terrain or the dead ball line, that is to say, when it is entirely beyond the boundary when viewed from directly above. A puddle, on which a jack floats freely, is considered to be an out of bounds area.

2) When, still on the authorised terrain, the moved jack is not visible from the circle, as defined in article 7. However, a jack masked by a boule is not dead. The umpire is authorised to temporarily remove a boule to declare whether the jack is visible.

3) When the jack is displaced to more than 20 metres (for Juniors and Seniors) or 15 metres (for the younger players) or less than 3 metres from the throwing circle.

4) When on marked out playing areas, the jack crosses more than one lane immediately to the side of the lane in use and when it crosses the end line of the lane.

5) When the displaced jack cannot be found, the search time being limited to 5 minutes.

6) When an out of bounds area is situated between the jack and the throwing circle.

7) When, in time limited games, the jack leaves the designated playing area

Article 10. Displacement of obstacles

It is strictly forbidden for players to press down, displace or crush any obstacle whatever on the playing area. However, the player about to throw the jack is authorised to test the landing point with one of their boules by tapping the ground no more than three times. Furthermore, the player who is about to play, or one of his partners, may fill in a hole which would have been made by one boule played previously.

For not complying with this rule, especially in the case of sweeping in front of a boule to be shot, the players incur the penalties outlined in article 35.

At the completion of an end, the last team to throw their boule <u>should</u> erase the circle/markings just played from, to restore the ground to its original condition so as not to affect future play.

Article 11. Changing of jack or boule.

Players are forbidden to change the jack or a boule during a game except in the following cases:

1) The one or the other cannot be found, the search time being limited to 5 minutes.

2) The one or the other is broken: in this case the largest part is taken into consideration. If boules remain to be played, it is immediately replaced, after measuring, if necessary, by a boule or a jack of identical or similar diameter. At the next end the player concerned can take a new complete set of boules.

(A player may not change their set of boules during the game if the original boules are undamaged and a warning will be given by the umpire)

JACK

Article 12, Jack masked or displaced.

If, during an end, a leaf or a piece of paper accidentally masks the jack these objects are removed.

If the jack comes to be moved by the wind or the slope of the terrain, for example or by an umpire, a player or spectator accidentally treading on it, a boule or a jack coming from another game, an animal or any other mobile object, it is returned to its original position, provided this was marked.

If the jack is moved by a boule played in this game, it is valid.

(This rule specifically refers to the jack being masked (from view) and does not allow a player to remove a stick or branch that is lying in the terrain but not masking the view of the jack.)

Article 13, Jack moved into another game.

If, during an end, the jack is displaced onto another terrain of play, marked out or not, the jack is valid subject to the conditions outlined in article 9.

(During a timed game the terrain string lines form the outer perimeters of play.)

The players using this jack will wait, if there is room, for the players in the other game to complete their end, before completing their own.

The players concerned by the application of this rule must show patience and courtesy.

At the following end the teams continue on the terrain which had been allotted to them and the jack is thrown again from the place it occupied when it was displaced, subject to the conditions of article 7.

(When the jack leaves the lane after being moved by a boule, the circle is returned to the position of the marked jack. If the jack was not marked or the mark cannot be agreed upon by both sides, the circle is placed inside the dead boule lines (side or back) where the jack left the lane. The circle can be moved back in line with the previous end's play, only to accommodate a valid throw between 6m to 10m. Many players believe they have a choice on where to place the circle (the original place of the marked circle or the place where the boule left the terrain). This rule clarifies that situation).

Article 14. Rules to apply if the jack is dead.

If, during an end, the jack is dead, one of three cases can apply:

1) Both teams have boules to play, the end is void and the jack is thrown by the team that scored the points in the previous end or who won the toss.

2) Only one team has boules left to play, this team scores as many points as boules that remain to be played.

3) The two teams have no more boules in hand, the end is void and the jack is thrown by the team that scored the points in the previous end or who won the toss.

Article 15. Positioning the jack after it has been stopped.

1) If the jack, having been hit, is stopped or deviated by a <u>spectator or by an umpire</u>, it remains in this position.

2) If the jack, having been hit, is stopped or deviated by a <u>player in the authorised playing area</u>, <u>his opponent has the choice of:</u>

a) leaving the jack in its new position;

b) putting it back in its original position;

c) placing it anywhere on the extension of a line going from its original position to the place that it is found, up to a maximum distance of 20 metres from the circle (15 metres for the younger players) and such that it is visible.

Paragraphs b) and c) can only be applied if the position of the jack was previously marked. If this was not the case, the jack will remain where it is found.

If, after having been struck, the jack travels into an out of bounds area before returning, finally, on to the playing area, it is classed as dead, and the actions defined in article 14 apply.

(If through playing a boule the jack is stopped by a player and remains on the valid lane and the jack was marked, the playing team/player can take the jack over the dead boule line as a dead jack (but not over 20 metres) and score as many points as they have boule in hand if the opposing team have no boules left to play. If the opposing team have boules left, the end can be pronounced dead by the playing team and a new end started with no points scored.)

BOULES

Article 16. Throwing of the first and following boules.

The first boule of an end is thrown by a player belonging to the team that has won the draw or has been the last to score. After that, it is the team that does not hold the point that plays.

The player must not use any object or draw a line on the ground to guide them in playing a boule or mark its landing point. Whilst playing their last boule, it is forbidden to carry a boule in the other hand.

The boules must be played one at a time.

Any boule thrown cannot be replayed. However, boules must be replayed if they have been stopped or deviated accidentally from their course between the <u>throwing circle and the jack</u> by a boule or jack coming from another game, or by an animal or any moving object (football, etc.) and in the case defined in article 8, third paragraph.

(Note: this article only applies if the boule is stopped or deviated between the circle and the jack!)

Before throwing his/her boule, the player must remove from it any trace of mud or whatever deposit, under threat of penalties outlined in article 35.

If the first boule played goes out-of-bounds, it is for the opponent to play first then alternately so long as there are no boules on the designated terrain.

If after shooting or pointing no boules are left on the designated playing area, the arrangements concerning a dead end as defined in article 29 apply.

(This rule is a nightmare for umpires. Example, team A plays a boule out of turn. So, does the boule that Team B then play also be interpreted as out of turn? There are numerous situations where boules can be deemed 'out of turn' and it will often come down to the umpire's application of 'common sense'.)

<u>Article 17. Behaviour of players and spectators during a game</u>

During the regulation time allowed for a player to throw a boule the spectators and players must observe total silence.

The opponents must not walk, nor gesticulate nor do anything that could disturb the player about to play. <u>Only their team-mate/s may remain between the throwing circle and the jack.</u>

The opponents must remain beyond the jack or behind the player and, in both cases, to the side with regard to the direction of play and at a distance of at least 2 metres the one from the other.

The players who do not observe these regulations could be excluded from the competition if, after a warning from an umpire, they persist in their conduct.

Article 18, Throwing of the boules and boules going outside the terrain.

Absolutely no-one, as a test, may throw their boules during a game including away from the lane where they are playing. Players who do not observe this rule could be penalised as set out in article 35.

During an end, boules going outside the marked terrain are valid except as in the application of article 19.

Article 19, Dead boules

Any boule is dead from the moment that it enters an out of bounds area. A boule straddling the boundary line of the authorised playing area is valid. The boule is dead only after having completely crossed the boundary of the allotted playing area, that is to say, when it is situated entirely beyond the boundary when viewed from directly above. The same applies when, on marked lanes, the boule completely crosses more than one of the lanes alongside the lane in use or when it crosses the end line of the lane.

In timed games played on a marked lane a boule is considered dead when it completely crosses the line of the designated lane.

If the boule comes back into the playing area, either because of the slope of the ground or by having rebounded from an obstacle, moving or stationary, it is immediately taken out of the game and anything that it has displaced after its passage into an out of bounds area is put back in place provided these objects have been marked.

Any dead boule must immediately be removed from the game. By default, it will be considered live the moment another boule is played by the opposing team.

(As an umpire, I ask the players to immediately remove any boules that are now considered dead-boules and put them over the dead boule line. As a player, it is a good habit to get into.)

Article 20, Stopped boules.

Any boule played that is stopped or deviated by a <u>spectator or an umpire, will remain where it comes to rest.</u>

Any boule played, that is stopped or deviated accidentally by a <u>player to whose team it belongs, is dead.</u>

Any boule pointed that is stopped or deviated accidentally by an <u>opponent, can, according to the wishes of the player, be replayed or left where it comes to rest.</u>

(Note the differences in the three situations noted above.)

When a boule shot, or hit is stopped or deviated accidentally by a player, the opponent may:

1) leave it where it stopped.

2) place it on the extension of a line which starts from the original position it occupied to its stopping point, but only on the playable area and only on condition that it had been marked.

The player purposely stopping a moving boule is immediately disqualified, along with their team, for the game in progress.

Article 21, Time allowed to play.

Once the jack is thrown each player has the maximum duration of one minute to play their boule. This short period starts from the moment when the previous boule or jack stops or, if it is necessary to measure a point, from the moment the latter has been carried out.

The same requirements apply to the throwing of the jack.

(So, the team winning the end has one minute to throw the Jack, from when the last boule has stopped or when points from the previous end have been agreed.)

All players not respecting this rule, incur the penalties outlined in article 35.

(If it is necessary to measure between the jack and the circle, the one minute is <u>*paused*</u> *during the time taken to measure, as when measuring boule positions. Be aware that your minute to play does not start again with a fresh time period of one minute.)*

When is an end deemed to be finished in timed games? This rule applies only in <u>*timed games*</u> *to determine how many ends remain to be played after the time signal is sounded. It is not used for any other purpose. When the time signal is sounded, players decide if all boules of the end have been played and have come to a stop. If so, that end has finished, (regardless of measuring and deciding points). It is the most objective point at which to decide the end of an end, as it does not allow players to 'play for time' through measuring, deciding points, calling the umpire etc. So, when the time signal is sounded...*

• If the last boule of the end has been played and come to a stop, you have officially started the new end and are therefore able to play that end, plus the tournaments official end(s).

• If the last boule of the end has NOT been played or NOT stopped, you finish that end and then play the tournament's official end(s).

Rules for an extra end in timed games:

When both teams are tied on equal score, either at the end of the time-period or after the extra end, a result must be obtained in the next end. <u>THE JACK MUST BE MARKED</u> and: a. If the jack is moved outside the playing area and both teams have boules in hand, the jack is returned to its original position and play continues. Any boules moved remain in their new position. b. If the jack is moved outside the playing area and both teams are out of boules, the jack is returned to its original position and the end is measured. Any boules moved remain in their new position. c. If only one team has boules left, this team scores as many points as boules that remain to be played as per article 14. Article 22. Displaced boules If a stationary boule is moved by the wind or slope of the ground, for example, it is put back).

Article 22. Displaced boules

If a stationary boule is moved by the wind or slope of the ground, for example, it is put back in its place, provided it has been marked. The same applies to any boule <u>accidentally displaced by a player, an umpire, a spectator, an animal or any moving object.</u>

To avoid any dispute, the players must mark the boules. No claim will be admissible for an unmarked boule, and the umpire will give a decision only in terms of the position the boules hold on the terrain.

(On a personal note, I have an issue here with the difference between the word 'must' and the word 'should'. By using the word 'must' it infers an

infraction of the rules which should be accompanied by a warning and a card. However, I have never seen any player given a warning for not marking their boule.)

(The marking of boules can only be carried out by a member of the playing team. The opponents can request that the playing team mark their boules, or that they be allowed onto the terrain to do so.)

However, if a boule is moved by a boule played in the same game, it remains in its new position.

Article 23. A player throwing a boule other than his own.

The player who plays a boule other than his own receives a warning. The boule played is nevertheless valid but must immediately be replaced, possibly after measuring has been done.

In the event of it occurring again during the game, the guilty player's boule is disqualified and anything it displaced is put back in place, if their positions were marked.

Article 24. Boules thrown contrary to the rules.

Except for cases in which these rules provide specific and graduated penalties as outlined in article 35, any boule thrown contrary to the rules is dead and if marked, anything that it has displaced in its travel is put back in place.

However, the opponent has the right to apply the advantage rule and declare it to be valid. In this case, the boule pointed or shot, is valid and anything it has displaced remains in its place.

(Boules played out of turn are deemed boules thrown contrary to the rules (contrary to Article 16)).

POINTS AND MEASURING

Article 25, Temporary removal of boules

In order to measure a point, it is permitted, after having marked their positions, to temporarily remove the boules and obstacles situated between the jack and the boules to be measured.

After measuring, the boules and the obstacles which were removed are put back in place. If the objects cannot be removed, the measuring is done with the aid of callipers.

(Under no circumstances must boules be twisted and turned on the surface to leave an indentation for the boule to be replaced in, or for the top of the boule to be hit by another boule. It is also forbidden to place a finger on a jack or boule to stop it from moving. To take any of these actions incurs a warning. If in doubt, call an umpire over as they usually have chocks or wedges to mark the boule positions. I'm told that the action of a boule being twisted in the ground to make an indentation can then make it harder for that particular boule to be moved by another shot. In the USA it appears to be permissible to tap a boule with another boule etc.)

Article 26, Measuring of points.

The measuring of a point is the responsibility of the player who last played or by one of their team-mates. The opponents always have the right to measure after one of these players.

Measuring must be done with appropriate instruments, which each team must possess.

Notably, it is forbidden to effect measurements with the feet. The players who do not observe this rule will incur the penalties outlined in article 35.

Whatever positions the boules to be measured may hold, and at whatever stage the end may be, an umpire can be consulted, and their decision is final. During the time that an umpire is measuring the players must be at least 2 metres away.

(It is important for the players to stand two meters away when the umpire is measuring. The last thing an umpire needs is an interested player eagle-eyed and kneeling down with the umpire while they measure a close call.)

By decision of the organising committee, especially in case of televised games, it may be decided that only an umpire is empowered to measure.

Article 27, Removed Boules

It is forbidden for players to pick up played boules before the completion of an end.

At the completion of an end, all boules picked up before the agreement of points are dead. No claim is admissible on this subject.

If a player picks up one of their boules from the playing area while his partners have boules remaining, they will not be allowed to play them.

(This includes boules behind the dead boule line, but not boules that have gone dead during play and need to be placed behind the dead ball line. Please do not touch the boules behind the dead boule line. Most teams will be counting the opponents remaining boules to determine their own play. So, picking up boules is at best a form of deceit. This is why the penalty for picking up a boule is so harsh!)

Article 28, Displacement of the boules or the jack

The team, whose player displaces or disturbs the jack or one of the contested boules, while effecting a measurement, loses the point.

(If a boule or jack is moved while effecting a measure, the team measuring loses the point, i.e. their boule is deemed to be not holding the point. The umpire should be called, and they will:

a) place the jack or boule to reflect the lost point if it has created an advantage to the team who moved the jack or boule.

b) If the movement has given the point to the opponents, it remains as it stands. The team losing the point must play the next boule.

This the main reason player should not offer to measure for the opponent. It's a lose-lose situation!)

If, during the measurement of a point, the umpire disturbs or displaces the jack or a boule, the umpire will make an impartial decision.

Article 29. Boules equidistant from the jack

When the two closest boules to the jack belong to opposing teams, and are at an equal distance from it, 3 cases can apply:

1) If the two teams have no more boules to play the end is dead and the jack belongs to the team which had scored the points in the previous end, or who had won the draw.

2) If only one team has boules at its disposition, it plays them and scores as many points as it has boules closer to the jack than the nearest opponent's boule.

3) If both teams have boules at their disposition, it is for the team which played the last boule to play again, then the opposing team, and so on alternately until the point belongs to one of them. When only one team possesses boules, the arrangements set out in the preceding paragraph apply.

If, after completion of the end, no boules remain within the authorised playing area, the end is null and void.

Article 30, Foreign bodies adhering to the boules or jack.

Any foreign bodies adhering to the boules, or the jack must be removed before measuring a point.

(This includes mud adhering to the boules.)

Article 31, Complaints

To be considered, any complaint must be made to an umpire.

(And the complaint must be made to the umpire during the playing of the game.)

As soon as the game is finished, no complaint can be accepted.

DISCIPLINE

Article 32, Penalties for absent teams or players

At the time of the draw and the announcement of its result, the players must be present at the control table. A quarter of an hour after the announcement of these results, the team which is absent from the terrain will be penalised one point which is awarded to their opponents. This time limit is reduced to 5 minutes in games that are timed.

After this time limit, the penalty accrues by one point for each five minutes of the delay. The same penalties apply throughout the competition, after each random draw.

If a game restart following an interruption, for any reason, the penalties will be one point for every 5 minutes the team is absent.

The team which does not present itself on the playing area within 30 minutes of the start or restart of games is declared to be <u>eliminated from the competition</u>.

An incomplete team has the right to start a game without waiting for its absent player; nevertheless, it does not use the boules of that player.

No player may be absent from a game or leave the playing area without the authorisation of an umpire. In any case this absence will not interrupt the course of the game, nor the obligation for the partners to play their boules in the specified minute. If the player has not returned by the time they are to play their boules, they are cancelled at the rate of one boule per minute.

(This rule applies when two Umpires are in attendance. When only one Umpire is in attendance, the departing player need only get the permission of their opposition. The requirement for time limited games still applies i.e. the player wanting to leave must have already played all their boules!)

If permission has not been granted the penalties outlined in article 35 shall apply.

In the case of an accident or medical problem officially recognised by a doctor, the player may be granted a maximum absence of fifteen minutes. If using this option should prove fraudulent, the player and his team will be immediately excluded from the competition.

<u>Article 33. Late arrival of players</u>

If, after an end has started, the missing player arrives, they do not take part in this end. The player is accepted into the game only as from the following end.

If a missing player arrives more than 30 minutes after the start of a game, they lose all rights to participate in that game.

If their team-mates win this game, the player will be able to participate in the following game provided they were originally registered with that team.

If the competition is played in pools[49], the player will be able to take part in the second game whatever the result of the first.

The first end of a game is considered as having started as soon as the jack has been thrown, regardless of the validity of the throw. The following ends are considered to have started as soon as the last boule from the previous end has stopped.

Article 34. Replacement of a player

The replacement of a player in Doubles, or of one or two players in Triples, is permitted before the official announcement of the commencement of the competition (gun, whistle, announcement, etc.), on condition that the substitute(s) was/were not previously registered in the competition as belonging to another team.

Article 35. Penalties

For non-observation of the rules during a game, the players incur the following penalties:

1) Warning, which is officially marked by an umpire presenting a yellow card to the player at fault.

However, a yellow card for exceeding the time limit will be imposed on all the players of the offending team. If one of these players has already been given a yellow card, they will be penalised by disqualification of the boule played or to be played.

---

49. https://petanquerules.wordpress.com/tournament-systems/#poules

2) Disqualification of the boule played or to be played, which is officially marked by an umpire presenting an orange card to the player at fault.

(Generally, most umpires will consider the offences to be of a cumulative nature. I.e, A yellow card for a first offence in a game and an orange (and subsequent boule disqualified) for the second offense in a game. Also be aware that a multitude of simultaneous offences can also incur a multitude of warning cards. That may mean two yellow cards or a yellow card <u>and</u> an orange card resulting in the loss of a boule. This circumstance would rarely occur but for example a player may have their rear foot over the circle and then also lift their foot while playing their boule or before the boule has landed).

3) Exclusion of the responsible player for the game, which is officially marked by an umpire presenting a red card to the player at fault.

4) Disqualification of the team responsible.

5) Disqualification of the two teams in case of complicity.

The warning is a sanction and can only be given after an infringement of the rules. Giving information to players or requesting they should respect the rules at the start of a competition or of a match is not to be considered as a warning.

(See Appendix 6)

(It should be noted that the giving of a warning (and yellow card) is not considered to a cumulative offence, so if you received a yellow card in game one you should get another yellow card for a similar level/technical offence in game two. However, if you get a second warning, in any single game, the next card you receive should be an orange card with the resultant disqualification of a boule to be played or a boule already played (depending on where the game is at). A red card should be preceded by

a yellow card and then an orange card for persistent offenders. However, it is at the umpire's discretion, so if an umpire believes the situation is sufficiently serious, the umpire can go straight to a red card.)

Article 36, Bad weather

In the event of inclement weather, such as heavy rain, any end started must be completed, unless a contrary decision is made by an umpire, who is the only person authorised, after consultation with the jury or organising committee, to make the decision to stop the games or, for the cancellation of the competition in the case of force majeure.

(Force Majeure would generally be interpreted as a lightning storm or strong and hazardous wind and weather conditions.)

Article 37, New phase of play

If, after the announcement to start a new phase of the competition (2nd round, 3rd round, etc.), certain games of the previous phase have not been completed, an umpire may, noting that the smooth running of the competition can no longer be assured, ask the jury or the organising committee to stop all outstanding games in progress or even the competition.

Article 38, Lack of Sportsmanship

The teams that argue during a game, who show lack of sportsmanship and respect towards the public, the organisers or the umpires, will be excluded from the competition. This exclusion can incur non-acceptance of the results, as well as the application of penalties set out in article 39.

(This article seems to determine the difference between a player who persistently ignores or flouts the rules and the player who is acting in a more serious (aggressive?) manner to other players or officials and the

penalties are more serious to reflect this worsening behaviour. Note also the explanation in an earlier chapter that indicates a player may be given a yellow card for unsportsmanlike behaviour and that yellow card is considered valid throughout the tournament. Subsequent offences may result in a red card being issued by the umpire and an automatic disqualification for the rest of the tournament.)

Currently there is discussion going on to denote that some penalties would be deemed 'technical offences' such as the one-minute rule or the stepping on the circle etc and some would be deemed 'behavioural offences' and the behavioural offences would probably be treated in a harsher manner than the technical offences.

Article 39. Bad behaviour

The player who is guilty of bad behaviour, or worse, violence towards an official, an umpire, another player or a spectator incurs one or several of the following penalties, depending on the seriousness of the offence.

1) Exclusion from the competition.

2) Withdrawal of licence or of the official document.

3) Confiscation or restitution of expenses and prizes.

The penalty imposed on the guilty player can also be imposed on their team-mates.

Penalty 1 is imposed by an umpire.

Penalty 2 is imposed by the jury or the organising committee.

Penalty 3 is imposed by the organising committee which, within 48 hours, sends a report with the expenses and prizes retained to the federation's organisation which will decide on their destination.

In all cases, the Chairman of the Committee for the Federation concerned will make the final decision.

Correct dress is required of the players, specifically it is forbidden to play without a top and for safety reasons, the players must wear fully enclosed shoes protecting the toes and heels.

It's forbidden to smoke during play, including electronic cigarettes. It is also forbidden to use mobile phones during the games.

(In most competitive games, it is also forbidden to drink alcohol! It is also an offence to listen to music through ear pods etc as it is deemed to be a safety issue for everyone.)

Any player who does not observe these rules, will be excluded from the competition if they persist after a warning from an umpire.

Article 40. Duties of the Umpires

The umpires designated to control the competitions are charged to be on the watch for strict application of the rules of play and the administration rules which complete them.

(Most umpires will have their 'pet peeves' which they are known for. Most umpires in the top-level games will exercise quite a tolerant attitude to the top players. So, when you see a top-level French game where the umpires are being tolerant with foot faults etc, don't expect that same latitude from your local umpire. I am told there other sets of rules to guide umpires in the televised competitions.)

Subject to the seriousness of the offence, they have the authority to exclude for a game or disqualify from the competition, any player or any team who refuses to comply with their decision.

The spectators with valid or suspended licences, who, by their behaviour, are the origin of incidents on the terrain of play, will be the subject of an umpire's report to the Federal executive. The latter will summon the guilty party or parties before a competent Disciplinary Committee who will decide on the penalties to apply.

Article 41, Composition and decisions of the Jury

Any case not provided for in the rules is submitted to an umpire who can refer it to the competition's jury. This jury comprises at least 3 people and at the most 5 people. The decisions taken by the jury in applying this paragraph are without appeal. In the case of a split vote, the president of the jury has the casting vote.

Chapter 13: Anecdotes about the game

Probably the most bizarre game I've ever played was in a Pub Garden in South Manchester. It was the middle of summer, and the garden was well populated by patrons who would get their carefully remembered drink tray from the bar and then walk back to their family and walk straight across the terrain! Speaking to the fellow players in our group, it seemed that it was inadvisable to berate the pub goers, especially as the Sunday session progressed and alcohol became more of a consideration. The local players had already worked out that it was a great venue to develop your 'Plombee shot'. We only played there the one time.

In Barcelona, Spain we looked out of our hotel window and spotted a Petanque terrain across the street. So, we wandered downstairs and over to the terrain. The locals were predominantly of an older age and spoke absolutely no English at all. By gestures we made out that we would love to have a game. Two of the players stepped off the terrain and gestured for us to use their boules. At the completion of the game, we said thanks, but another two players stepped off the terrain and gestured for us to use their boules. This was repeated for the rest of the evening. I should be more specific here and say that these players were for the most part quite old! Quite a few of them had no teeth. Between us and the language barrier we had a great evening and were invited to join them for a beer afterwards. I think one thing that endeared us to them was the fact that we were from New Zealand, and they had never seen a kiwi before! Over the beer they seemed to be inviting us to come again, the next evening. One thing I remember well is the amount of laughter that went on. The next night we went along on the off chance that we had correctly interpreted their Invitation. On this night, they had actually brought along a couple of sets of spare boules. Now that our playing skills had been demonstrated we were on a par with these players and the games became a little more serious, but I mainly remember the laughter. I remember once taking out my wife's boule when I was shooting (it happens!) much to their amusement. Me, being the showman, I bowed to them in a mock effort to get their applause. They redoubled their laughter and for the rest of the stay in Barcelona, whenever anyone made a dud shot, it became incumbent on them to bow while we all laughed loudly!

I once played at hanging Rock just outside of Adelaide in Australia. yes, it was very hot but that was not the main problem.

The Kangaroos were the main problem! They would come and sit in the shade on the terrain and go to sleep. I may have mentioned that I was scared of snakes etc to one of the locals, so every time my boule went into the undergrowth, I was warned about the type of snake that preferred to live under that very type of undergrowth. Yes, it was all very good natured, but it is still a little bit of a worry when Snakes bug you as much as they bug me! Don't get me wrong, there is a rivalry between the Aussies and the Kiwis, but it is very good natured, and I'd do exactly the same when they visit our shores. When the kangaroos came and parked on the terrain and the locals were saying I shouldn't be doing anything to aggravate them, I assumed they were winding me up again. I'd watched Skippy on TV as a kid. Kangaroos were friendly!

When I went to shoo one of them off the terrain, a couple of locals grabbed me and repeated their warning. Evidently Kangaroos are not all like Skippy! They can be quite aggressive. Whoops. It seems that the most sensible thing to do with a kangaroo parked on your terrain, sunbathing, is to move to another terrain! Well, that lesson was well learned!

When we visited France, I was quite keen to see what I assumed would be petanque terrains everywhere. Below the Eiffel Tower was a huge terrain which was sadly populated by everything but petanque players. Never mind! As we headed to Le Mans (another passion of mine) we saw a notice that pointed off towards the local petanque terrain. We carried on convinced we were now in Petanque Country and never saw another terrain! Just a little disappointing!

Favourite terrain of mine would have to be the terrain at Rotorua, in the Government gardens. The setting is magnificent with the Tudor towers as the background. The handy bowling club is a very friendly place to get a drink afterwards. I was a member there for over ten years until an injury forced me to step away from the game.

My next favourite would be the terrain at Wanganui East.

It is a very soft surface topped with 'pea metal' which is very forgiving. The club next door is a very friendly club and a handy place to get a drink afterwards. The membership is very welcoming and quite competitive and they usually have a good turnout when travelling to local competitions etc.

The Photo below was taken while I was running a coaching session for some of the local club members. As I said, it's a very welcoming club and quite competitive

. And my third favourite terrain would be the set up at the hanging Rock near Adelaide. A great bunch of locals who ribbed me mercilessly about my fear of snakes but also saved me from going too close to the Kangaroos who can be a bit moody!

Representing New Zealand.

It was an amazing honour and in that particular year, it was the last year where the top 8 teams from the National triple's tournament were invited to a weekend tourney to decide who would represent NZ. Six games were played on the Saturday, and we were drawn to play the favourites on our first game on Sunday Morning. It was a close game, but we won! I have no idea who was making the draw, but we ended up playing the team of favourites twice more on that Sunday before we ended up as declared victors. The hugs and handshakes we received from the team of favourites were both genuine and heartfelt.

My Favourite Frenchman is a guy called 'C' and he is a really lovely guy who had played on the team of favourites that we beat three times to get to New Caledonia. He decided to come on the trip to New Caledonia with us and it was a boon that he did. In New Caledonia most of the announcements were only made in French so having 'C' around came in very handy.

During the shooting competition, at which I finished down the field, and wandered off to get lunch. 'C' came running up and grabbed me. "There is a playoff for sixteenth place between you and the new Caledonian shooter. You must hurry up!" Because the announcements were all in French, I'd taken no notice.

I wandered back to the Shooting competition and the New Caledonian Shooter was wandering around the piste saying something in French that I could not understand. 'C' offered a translation. "He says he eats Kiwis for his breakfast!" He missed his first two shots and I hit both of mine. When I asked 'C' for the French translation of "So how's your breakfast going down?" 'C' correctly suggested I get on with the shooting. I did win the shootout and went on to finish around twelfth in the rankings. We had an amazing time in New Caledonia, which is where we were introduced to the concept of betting on games of Petanque. On the Sunday we had gone down to the local Pistes to get some practice in. One of our younger team members fancied having a go with some of the locals. He changed his mind when he was told that the buy in for this game was approx. four hundred euros!

A couple of days later this same young guy and I were practicing on a spare terrain when an older Polynesian guy and what looked like his seven-year-old grandson approached and asked for a game. We were fine with that until he suggested a side bet of $200. Remember this guy had been watching us practice for a while and then wanted to put money on the game. We politely declined.

It was a strict rule that people were not allowed to bet on the games in the tournament. I did notice that no sooner had a game finished in the tournament that those same players would wander off to the practice terrains and have another game. I can't help feeling that some serious cash changed hands on those practice terrains!

Lastly. We were playing in one of the local tournaments back in Auckland and we were playing 'C's' wife. 'R' was a really lovely lady and a great help in New Caledonia.

Jane and I were having one of those ends where we could not get a boule within a meter of the Jack. It happens. And although you try your best to not get disappointed it's still a nuisance. R's team got all of their boules comfortably inside ours and we (begrudgingly) conceded six points. That was not enough for 'R'. she wanted to measure for the next point. I tried to put a smile on my face and said it was stupid. She insisted so I lost the smile and said, "I think there's something in the rules that says you are limited to just six points per end because that's the amount of boules you have played!" She opened her mouth to protest again and then realised what was going on. She apologised. Did I mention she was a blonde?

'R' died a year or so later and she was dearly missed. She was a real stalwart in the Petanque Community. 'C' is still playing alongside us and is still a great member of the Petanque community in New Zealand.

And last but by no means least, who is my favourite doubles partner? That would have to be my lovely wife, Jane. We represented New Zealand together and she has put up with all of my days when the terrain has been to blame for all that is wrong with the world. Yes, we have won a few prizes along the way, but I still count her as my biggest win so far!

Chapter 14: Umpire Questions.

<u>*Chapter 1 Question:*</u>

The situation is this. The Jack is thrown over the side string to the next lane by your opponents who said it is fine as it is an untimed game.

See Article 6 of the rules.

If the lane has been designated by the organisers, the jack must be thrown on this lane. The teams concerned must not go to a different lane without the umpire's permission. In this situation, the jack should be handed to your team who can then place it on the terrain at a position of your choosing.

<u>**Chapter 2 question:**</u>

Team A captain picked up the jack believing that all boules had been played. However, Team B still had a boule left to play. The jack was not marked, so I know the player who threw it should receive a yellow card. But what about Team B who is still holding a boule?

See Article 6

The Jack is put back approximately where it was, and team B plays its boules. If the teams cannot agree on the position of the Jack, team B will be allowed to position the Jack back to where it was. It's an axiom with umpires that the team making the mistake should not profit from that mistake. The player who did not mark the Jack should receive a warning as should the team B player who picked up the jack

<u>**Chapter 3 question:**</u>

Team A throws an illegal jack.

Team B picks up the circle, takes it back approx. 1 metre and proceeds to throw the jack from the circle. The jack lands in the middle of the piste and it is pointed out to the player of Team B, by one of its team, that he should 'place' the jack. The player firstly moves the circle back and then picks up the jack again and places it on the edge of the piste, right next to the string.

Is it legal for a team to place a jack twice?

See Article 6:

There are three issues here. In the first issue of the player, from Team B, throwing the jack from the circle, the player should get a warning for throwing the jack illegally (it should be <u>placed</u> in its new position). The second issue becomes the matter of whether the opposing team can place the jack again and the answer to this question is yes. Again, see Article 6.

The third issue is that of moving the circle backwards. Yes, it is legal for the opposing team to move the circle backwards providing they do it before they place the jack on the terrain.

<u>Chapter 4 question:</u>

Team A throws the first boule thrown after the game starts.

Immediately, Team B shot this boule, and the two boules went out-of-bounds. There are no boules left on the terrain.

Which team should throw the boule next, A or B

As there are no boules left on the terrain, team B should throw the next boule, which will then be followed by Team A until a boule is holding closest to the jack and within the playing area.

Chapter 5 Umpire Question

Team A throws the jack and it is just under the 6.00 meter mark by twenty centimeters. Team B say they are quite happy to play the jack as it lies. Can they do this?

No, the rules clearly stipulate that the jack must be between 6 and 10 meters from the inside of the circle.

Chapter 6 Umpire question.

Players are not allowed to smoke or drink alcohol etc during a game. What about a player eating some food?

Eating food during a game is allowed and is not mentioned in the rules.

<u>Chapter 7 Umpire question:</u>

This is a tricky one that happened when I was an umpire. Team A threw their first boule. Team B threw their first boule. Team A Captain who was standing by the head indicated that team B were holding and gestured to his team mate to throw the next boule. Team A threw all of their five remaining boules without disturbing the Jack or the two initial boules that were thrown. Team B then threw their five remaining boules, again without disturbing the Jack or the two initial boules thrown.

When the team captain of Team A looked again at the head, he decided to measure the head and as a result awarded one point to team A.

I was stood on the footpath by the terrain, so I had a very good view of the complete end.

In the end the team captain of team B, to avoid a fuss, conceded the point. As I was not called onto the piste by either team my input was not asked for. If I had been called onto the terrain, using the axiom that the team making the mistake should not then make a profit from the situation, I would have given the point to the team B.

How would you have handled it?

Question for chapter 8

A Player inadvertently throws a teammates boule. Does that boule count?

See Article 23

The player who plays a boule other than his own receives a warning. The boule played is nevertheless valid but must immediately be replaced, possibly after measuring has been done.

In the event of it occurring again during the game, the guilty player's boule is disqualified and anything it displaced is put back in place, if their positions were marked.

Question for chapter 9

One of your opponents is wearing gloves. Is that allowed?

It is not actually covered in the rules, but it is allowed! Most people would hold that the wearing of gloves would give no advantage other than keeping your hands warm.

Question for Chapter 10

Does an umpire have to first give a yellow card as a warning for bad behaviour, or can they go straight to a red card if the offence is sufficient to merit that punishment?

See rule 39. The umpire uses his or her discretion entirely in determining if the offence is sufficiently serious to warrant issuing a red card. There is no appeal for this offence. If the player was part of a team, the other players can continue to play but may not play the excluded players boules. Also, the red card may also be issued to the entire team if the offence warrants such action.

Question for Chapter 11

This happened to me when I was an umpire. The Jack was travelling along the string having been hit by a boule. One team were convinced it had gone over the line and the other team were equally convinced it had not gone over.

I was called in and explained that my decision could only reflect the position of the Jack and boules as they lay. The Jack was in a valid position on the terrain, so I called it accordingly. Both teams accepted my decision.

Now I wax eloquently about the joys of umpiring!

Seriously, it is not a bad job. You get to meet nearly all the players on the terrain. For the most part you have the respect of the players and because you are umpiring, less players will try dodgy rulings on you. On the upside your word is the law for that day. On the downside, you may well have to give a player or two a warning etc.

For me, Umpiring has always been a small way of giving something back to the sport that has given me so much fun over the years. Often, as a player, I will be asked for my interpretation of a ruling which is always a little boost to the ego. Now I ask you to consider becoming an umpire. The training is not overly arduous. For the initial club umpires exam, I was asked to go online and sit through around 3 hours of Zoom training and then take the exam. The exam was an 'Open book' type of exam which means you can have a set of the rules available to you for consultation. I was also fortunate that Mike Pegg, the Senior UK umpire was coming to Australia to run an umpire course. So, a friend and I went over to do the course and also play in a local tourney or two (Avoca and Hanging Rock).

Mike was a great guy to deal with and very informative in passing on his knowledge. So, I qualified and then went on to work with Andre Deramond at an international event in New Zealand. There really have been some amazing times as an umpire and I am so glad I took that step.

For now, I mainly just umpire at a local or regional level and here is where I ask you, as a reader, to step in.

In my club there are eight players who have taken the umpire exam. At a worst case scenario, I may only miss one in eight tourneys at my local club when it becomes my turn to be the umpire. Occasionally I am asked to umpire at a neighboring club event. In return they may send one of their members to oversee one of our events.

Worst case scenario is that I may do a couple or three tourneys a year where I have a quiet day and watch the other players while being called on for the odd measure or rule interpretation etc. The benefits as a player are that you become confident in your rule interpretations and few people will try and pull the wool over your eyes. There is also the benefit that players will treat you with some respect because they recognize you as a knowledgeable player. And the last but not least benefit is that you are giving something back to the game which has given you so much!

Try it!

Acknowledgements:

Firstly a huge thank you to my lovely wife Jane who has watched and encouraged as I tried to find the better/easier way to play the great game And also for continuing to proof read the finished article (Every time I refinished the manuscript).

A big thanks to Anne Peck, (The Wanganui East club president) who cast her eye over the finished product and made some excellent suggestions.

A huge thanks to Mike Pegg and Andre Deramond for their continued work in supporting the Umpires of our game.

Thanks to Trevor for being my practice partner over the years and for supplying some of the photos.

Thanks to the New Zealand Petanque association for giving me access to the rules etc and helping me become a better Umpire.

Jane either supplied the photos or was the model in many of the photos used.

And last but by no means least, thanks to all of the wonderful players I have met across the world and more especially here in New Zealand. Many of you I will remember with fondness.

It's been great!

I look forward to catching up with you again, on the piste!

Also available by this Author.

Soul Purpose

Vol 1 & 11 & 111

A fiction work with something of a twist. We have heard of reincarnation, right? It's something to laugh about, right? What if it is happening here. What if it is happening right in front of you?

Maybe you should read the book and find out about it. It's not as scary as you think. Or is it?

He has returned.

The subtitle is "and it's so not what you think" Probably one of the most fun books I have written and probably the most amusing. The Son of God has returned, and he finds the world is in something of a state. Partly because of what he said and did a couple of thousand years ago on his last visit here. Yeah, it's all a bit confused now he is back. Let's see how he deals with it!

Mickey Carter: An angel with L-plates

It's funny and set in South Manchester. It's easy being an angel. Isn't it?

I have Angels at my table.

An interesting story set in England as natural disasters occur and the higher levels of heaven are involved.

Danny Casanova's legacy

A fun story centred around a young guys first venture into the world of grownups and doing what grownups do. Or at least trying to!

Time and time again.

A book about past life experiences. Interestingly it only deals with past lives on planet earth.

Police series

A series about crime in 'Rotorua'

Book1 The Panel

It's an interesting story. What if, when you end up in court, there is a panel that sits independently and decides if you have received sufficient punishment. If it thinks you haven't, it does something about it! Yes, it may be a yarn, at this point!

Book 2 The Party

So, there's a party and it's one of those parties where clothes and inhibitions don't count for a lot. And then it turns out as a murder case. It gets very real for DS Hammell who accidentally gets invited to the party!

Book 3 The Judge

So, we have a zealot who thinks he is there to pass judgement on Girls who dress 'loosely'. DS Mark Hammell has to work out who this guy is and then there is a copycat crim also working the streets of Rotorua. Who has done what and which case is where?

Book 4 The War

A gang war breaks out in town DS Hammell has to settle the territories and also be on one side while pretending he is on neither side. Well at least the Chinese group are not involved. Or are they?

Book 5 The payoff.

It's a time when friendships are tested on the streets of Rotorua. 'It's not an easy time for DS Hamell. Then it gets very personal!

About the Author

Andy has been writing for the last twenty years and has written a number of books over a wide variety of genre. His first book Sold over 5000 copies and he continues to write on whatever the mood takes him. Currently he is finishing Books on the crime scene in Rotorua, New Zealand. As always his books are not meant to be taken seriously. If you haven't laughed today, read one of Andy's books!

www.ingramcontent.com/pod-product-compliance
Lightning Source LLC
Chambersburg PA
CBHW061341160726
47995CB00001B/117